ENDOR

Capital punishment is an emotion... , ... , tematically examines the historical background of the issue and then, more importantly, examines the objections and the scriptures to present a compelling argument. As a practicing attorney and as a retired Marine Lieutenant Colonel, I fully endorse his scathing criticism of our liberal activist judges. Dr. Gleason's book has settled the issue for me and I challenge those on both sides of the issue to read it.

Richard B. Hudson, J.D.
Fallbrook, CA

The Death Penalty on Trial will challenge both sides of the capital-punishment debate to know and articulate their positions more definitively. Dr. Gleason presents an incisive overview of capital punishment, with careful cautions on interpreting specific events in their proper context. He avoids simplistic answers to this serious topic, recognizing that real lives are at stake. This book assesses and provides clear guidance for establishing and maintaining a safe and righteous society.

Dr. Dominic A. Aquila
President, New Geneva Theological Seminary, Colorado Springs, CO

Fuzziness on ethical issues is the bane of modern thinking. Happily, there is a voice of clear reason on the scene. Dr. Ron Gleason brings genuine moral clarity to the issue of capital punishment by his illuminating survey of American History. The reader will be most appreciative of Dr. Gleason's masterful discussion of the objections to the death penalty. This book is a must-read for all lawyers, judges, and law officers.

Pastor Carl Robbins
Senior Minister, Woodruff Road Presbyterian Church
Greenville, SC

Regardless of one's own position on the controversial issue of capital punishment, Dr. Gleason clearly and effectively gives readers the resources to work through this topic and equips them to discuss it with others. This powerful book will make a significant contribution to this topic. I recommend it for careful reading, study, and discussion.

Dr. Charles Dunahoo
Coordinator of PCA Christian Education and Publications
Atlanta, GA

THE
DEATH PENALTY
ON TRIAL

TAKING A LIFE
FOR
A LIFE TAKEN

THE
DEATH PENALTY
ON TRIAL

TAKING A LIFE
FOR
A LIFE TAKEN

Ron Gleason, Ph.D.

Nordskog Publishing inc.

Ventura, California
2008

The Death Penalty on Trial: Taking a Life for a Life Taken
published by
Nordskog Publishing Inc.

© 2008 by Ron Gleason, Ph.D.
Second Printing 2009

International Standard Book Number: 978-0-9796736-7-2

Library of Congress Control Number: 2009921183

Cover Image, *Lady Justice*: Photo © 2009 JupiterImages Corporation.
Used by permission. All rights reserved.

Unless otherwise indicated, all Scripture quotations are from:
The Holy Bible, English Standard Version®.
Copyright ©2001 by Crossway Bibles, a publishing ministry of Good News Publishers.
Used by permission. All rights reserved.

Appendix:
Reprinted from *How Would Jesus Vote? A Christian Perspective on the Issues,* ©2001.
CHAPTER 5: Crime and Punishment: Judging the Death Penalty
by D. James Kennedy, Ph.D. and Jerry Newcombe, D.Min.
Used by permission of authors, and WaterBrook Press, Colorado Springs, CO.
All rights reserved.

Editor and Interior Design, Desta Garrett
Book Cover Design, Aaron Ford
Theology Editor, Ronald Kirk
Proofreader, Kimberley Winters Woods
Manuscript Editor, Bayard Taylor

Printed in the United States of America.

NORDSKOG PUBLISHING, INC.
2716 Sailor Ave., Ventura, California 93001 USA
1-805-642-2070 • 1-805-276-5129
www.NordskogPublishing.com

Christian Small Publishers Association

TABLE OF CONTENTS

Dedication   ix

The Publisher's Word   xi

DEDICATION

To the congregation of Grace Presbyterian Church
in Yorba Linda, California.

You'll never know how much you mean to me and my family.
May our gracious Lord continue to bless you richly
and may you grow daily in your understanding
of His Word and its application in your life!

THE PUBLISHER'S WORD

"You shall not murder."
(Deuteronomy 5:17)

*"The LORD... comes to judge the earth. He will
judge the world in righteousness, and
the peoples in His faithfulness."*
(Psalm 96:13)

THIS BOOK is primarily written to Christians, as the author proposes Biblical answers to the question of capital punishment. But this book is applicable to all people in all places for all time, as the matter of God's Sixth Commandment and the just punishment of its transgressors is of vital importance to everyone's life and safety today and forever.

Routinely we hear news of judicial decisions where cold-blooded murderers are given lax sentences by lenient judges and juries due to their false assumption that evil-doers in society can, over time, somehow be rehabilitated while locked-up in prisons. Or that a life taken unjustly does not warrant the penalty of taking another life – the life of the perpetrator of this most vicious of all crimes.

Consequently, our jails are excessively clogged with criminals including the worst of all, murderers, because the decision-makers sitting on benches in courtrooms think they are able to mete out legal penal punishment and sanctions more judicially and wisely than the Creator of life Himself.

The Death Penalty On Trial: The Taking of a Life for a Life Taken examines the pros and cons of this crucial issue in our culture; the reasons propounded in the public square for measuring guilt and the perceived appropriate penalties regarding the issue of killing, specifically of murder. This issue is hugely important for the protection of innocent lives and the overall safety in the current worldwide culture of death.

The author addresses and responds to all the main arguments in opposition to capital punishment, as well as those thoughtful reasons for carefully implementing the death penalty as appropriate for proven cases of guilt in a court of law for murderers committing this most heinous of all crimes (the worst of all sins according to God's Word).

Most secularists and many Christians adhere to the false hope of rehabilitation and the erroneous opinion that the taking of a life by execution for a life taken by murder is unnecessary and unwarranted – or even cruel and inhumane. Some even go so far as to say that the death penalty is every bit as horrific as the innocent victim's murder.

There are hundreds of opinions on many complex issues in the world today. Every person has a viewpoint, and generally it is to do what is right in his or her own eyes. On this particular controversy, there must be a best, right-approach solution. This issue is critical for the safety and well-being of society as a whole, which includes the victims and their families as well as the criminal. So which stance is the correct one?

Today the death penalty is on trial around the world. Rarely are convicted murderers put to a speedy death following a speedy trial. Most linger in jail for years, many are released early on parole, and some commit more serious crimes, including murdering additional victims (recidivism).

Let's dissect the critical points of this monumental matter. We are to love and not harm our neighbor, since men and women are created in the image of God and He admonishes us, "You Shall Not Murder." Our Creator tells us of His requirements of a just and proper penalty. Shouldn't we heed our most wise and loving Maker?

Please consider Dr. Gleason's case and come to your own conclusion, but do so carefully and with an open mind after having reviewed all the arguments, positions, and rebuttals. Digest this  book fully. This publisher and the author, Dr. Ron Gleason, believe God's penal antidote for this terrible act of evil-doing is the "Taking of a Life – for a Life Taken," according to Holy Scriptures.

— Gerald Christian Nordskog

January 2009

1

INTRODUCTION

IF someone asks you why you support the death penalty, especially if you are a Christian, can you give coherent reasons for the position you take on this controversial ethical issue? If you cannot, then this book may give you a deeper understanding of the debate. My aim is to challenge you to develop your mind and your understanding about this important and controversial issue so that you are equipped to explain capital punishment from a moral, historical, and Biblical perspective. Simultaneously, there are other layers to examine in order to accomplish my goals for this book.

Not too long ago, I received a brochure from a group of religious leaders, both Jewish and Protestant, announcing an anti-death-penalty conference. This book is also meant to speak to all those who are ostensibly from a broad Judeo-Christian background who believe that the Bible does not allow for capital punishment.

Finally, this book is designed to engage those from a non-theistic background who wish to dialogue about how Christians can be pro-life and pro-death-penalty at the same time.

Biblical Foundations

It is prudent to begin by defining *Christian ethics*. All ethics have to do with human conduct. Christian ethics, however, conforms to a divine, absolute standard. In other words,

> The special concern of Christian ethics is to relate an understanding of God to the conduct of men and women and, more specifically, to explore the response to God which Jesus Christ requires....[1]

That is to say, Christians are bound to and by Scripture as the standard by which all decisions and conduct are measured. What, concretely, constitutes Christian ethics? Allow me to give you three directives: First, Christian ethics is a God-centered approach that uses Scripture to point us to the revealed will of God for man *and* how man must respond to God's revealed will in a changing world; secondly, Christian ethics is derived from strongly developed as well as practically applied systematic and Biblical theologies that are Christ-centered and Christ-honoring; and, thirdly, Christian ethics serve as a guide for us to *think* and *act* wisely, by which I mean in a Spirit-guided and Spirit-empowered manner, in the unfolding circumstances of our daily lives. In short, Christian ethics is based on a recognition of the authority, wisdom, and goodness of God as Creator over man the creature, based on the Biblical teaching that man is created in the image of God (*imago Dei*), and that Christians are called to think God's thoughts after Him.

Our next step is twofold. It is to encourage a thoroughly Biblical understanding of the character of God and the consistency and authority of the whole Word of God. Not all Christians have the same practical view of the infallibility and inerrancy of Scripture or how the Bible should be interpreted. In order to help explain and support the important point of Biblical interpretation, I will provide illustration representing some of the most rigorously defended Biblical traditions as seen in the Westminster Confession of Faith and the Belgic Confession.

In the Westminster Confession of Faith 1.4 we read,

> The authority of the Holy Scripture, for which it ought to be believed, and obeyed, depends not upon the testimony of any man, or church; but wholly upon God (who is truth itself) the author thereof; and therefore it is to be received, because it is the Word of God.

In terms of interpretation and how we go about gleaning the necessary material to make a Biblical decision about an issue, Westminster Confession of Faith 1.6 states,

> The whole counsel of God concerning all things necessary for His own glory, man's salvation, faith, and life, is either expressly set down in Scripture, or by good and necessary consequence may be deduced from Scripture: unto which nothing at any time is to be added, whether by new revelations, or the Spirit, or traditions of men.

The Belgic Confession (1567; author Guido de Brès) said this in Article 7 (The Sufficiency of the Holy Scriptures to Be the Only Rule of Faith):

> We believe that those Holy Scriptures fully contain the will of God, and that whatsoever man ought to believe unto salvation is sufficiently taught therein. For since the whole manner of worship which God requires of us is written in them at large, it is unlawful for any one, though an apostle, to teach otherwise than we are now taught in the Holy Scriptures: *nay, though it were an angel from heaven,* as the apostle Paul says. For since it is forbidden to *add unto or take away anything from the Word of*

God, it does thereby evidently appear that the doctrine thereof is most perfect and complete in all respects.

Neither may we consider any writing of men, however holy these men may have been, of equal value with those divine Scriptures, nor ought we to consider custom, or the great multitude, or antiquity, or succession of times and persons, or councils, decrees or statutes, as of equal value with the truth of God, since the truth is above all; *for all men are of themselves liars, and more vain that vanity itself.* Therefore we reject with all our hearts whatsoever does not agree with this infallible rule which the apostles have taught us, saying, *Prove the spirits, whether they are of God. Likewise: If any one comes to you, and doesn't bring this teaching, do not receive him in your house. (Emphasis added.)*

These confessional statements provide us with a foundational statement of the authority of Scripture, as well as how it is to be interpreted. The guidelines of Scripture, the Westminster Standards, and the Belgic Confession will be traceable throughout this book. I understand that not everyone within Christianity has studied or adopted these confessions, but to the extent committed Christians are faithful in interpreting the Bible, they would likely be in general agreement with these pronouncements.

For the secularists, I would simply state that these are sources that many Christians use in their decision-making process. It is a combination of what the Bible says and what the Christian tradition has handed down to us in the way of sound Biblical interpretation.

In Genesis, chapter 1, we read of a holy, powerful God who created human beings, both male and female, in His own image, to have dominion over other creatures, and to hold to a thoroughly Scriptural notion of the sanctity of human life (cf. Gen. 9:5-6; Rom. 13:1-4). Attached to the understanding of the *imago*

Dei is the concomitant concept of the Creator/creature distinction and the lordship of God over all of life.

Definitions can be useful tools to set the table for what is coming. Therefore, I'll begin with a simple definition and then expand on that to include two other, more comprehensive ones. The first short definition comes from American Calvinist theologian John M. Frame's work on ethics. He writes, "Ethics is theology, viewed as a means of determining which persons, acts, and attitudes receive God's blessing and which do not."[2] The Dutch ethicist, Jochem Douma, wrote "Dogmatics without ethics is empty; ethics without dogmatics is blind."[3] The word "doctrine" or the words "Biblical doctrine" can supplant Douma's use of the word "Dogmatics." I will make the same adjustment to the last definition of the relationship between the *credena* of life (what we believe) and the *agenda* (what we do). The final definition is taken from the *Reformed Dogmatics* of Herman Bavinck (Dutch theologian, who died in 1921). Here is what he wrote:

> Dogmatics describes the deeds of God done for, to, and in human beings; ethics describes what renewed human beings now do on the basis of and in the strength of those divine deeds. In dogmatics human beings are passive; they receive and believe; in ethics they are themselves active agents. In dogmatics the articles of the faith are treated; in ethics, the precepts of the Decalogue. In the former, that which concerns faith is dealt with; in the latter, that which concerns love, obedience, and good works. Dogmatics sets forth what God is and does for human beings and causes them to know God as their Creator, Redeemer, and Sanctifier; ethics sets forth what human beings are and do for God now; how, with everything they are and have, with intellect and will and all their strength, they devote themselves to

go out of gratitude and love. Dogmatics is the system
of the knowledge of God; ethics is that of the service
of God. The two disciplines, far from facing each other
as two independent entities, together form a single system; they are related members of a single organism.[4]

All three of these definitions will serve us well in the course of
this book. The last, although somewhat extensive, clearly points
to the inextricable relationship between doctrine and conduct.

When it comes to the ethical issue of capital punishment, the
foregoing translates into a careful investigation of what Scripture
teaches rather than a mere personal opinion on the subject. For
instance, even though Scripture points in the direction of a very
high view of man as created in the image of God, it also makes
a clear distinction between killing and murder, as we shall see
in more detail later. Killing is not only allowed, but, at times,
commanded, while murder is condemned. The perpetrator of
the latter was to receive the loss of his or her life (*lex talionis*).
In the Old Testament in particular, the command to put to
death the one committing murder was accompanied with the
refrain "and thus you shall purge the evil from your midst." In
our approach to the death penalty as Christians, therefore, we
must continually remember what the Bible teaches about the
image-bearing nature of humans and the Image-Giving nature of
God (cf. Gen. 1:26–28). The crime of murder is heinous precisely
because *every human being bears the image of God.* Someone
who strikes down the image-bearer strikes at the holy, almighty
Image-Giver, God Himself.

With that said, we are ready to proceed.

2

A HISTORICAL

OVERVIEW

APART from directives found in the Old Testament, capital punishment was first written into a secular code of law around 1750 B.C. when The Code of Hammurabi applied the death penalty to approximately twenty-five offenses. In addition, Assyrian law (1500 B.C.), the legal code of the Hittite community (around 1400 B.C.), and the laws of ancient Egypt (approximately 1500 B.C.), sentenced convicted criminals to death by execution for certain crimes.[1] Thus, we see that it was not only the Israelites (from whom we trace the Christian faith) but also other surrounding pagan nations or cultures mentioned in the Bible who included the death penalty in their legal systems. We should not conclude that capital punishment is validated by virtue of the fact that the pagan nations surrounding Israel also had the death penalty. It is noteworthy, however, that even pagan nations exercised capital punishment against convicted murderers.

In ancient Athens, murder, defacing coins, certain cases of theft, kidnapping, and picking someone's pocket were deemed crimes worthy of death.[2] In the early Roman Empire, the military made use of capital punishment and later, when Roman leaders realized that the death penalty was, in fact, a deterrent, the public execution of prisoners became common. The methods of execution were crucifixion, decapitation, and burning. The evil emperor, Nero, misused his authority by using capital punishment as a means of entertainment in the arena rather than as an outworking of justice. Many Christians became the "entertainment" and were murdered because of their faith during his reign.

In the course of church history, during the Middle Ages especially, some Popes opposed capital punishment and two early councils of the Christian Church, the Council of Toledo (A.D. 675) and the Fourth Lateran Council (A.D. 1215), forbade the clergy to participate in capital judicial trials.[3] Most recently, both Pope John Paul II (elected October 1978) and Pope Benedict XVI (April 2005) have been outspoken against the death penalty.

Most of the Protestant Reformers were proponents of capital punishment. The rise of those in favor of the death penalty during the Reformation is connected with Renaissance scholarship, Biblical preaching, renewed interest in exegesis, and a grasp of the Biblical doctrine of God's covenant with man. All of these taken together helped formulate a clearer Biblical picture of the difference between murder and killing. Both Luther and Calvin, for example, favored the death penalty as we shall see when we perform a brief reconnaissance of the discussions surrounding capital punishment in the history of the church. Both men favored the execution of wicked men when justice required it. What would constitute "justice" for them? In short, there were two areas where they looked. First, for both Luther and Calvin, Scripture would be their primary guide regarding when they would approve of capital punishment. Second, they would look to natural law as an adjunct to what Scripture taught. This is not to say that natural law was needed to support Scripture. Quite the contrary, Scripture took precedence over everything and everyone. Francis Nigel Lee, PH.D., TH.D., wrote,

> The Moral Laws of God, as expressed in the Ten Com-
> mandments, are all-embracing in their scope. In all ages,
> they are central for man as the very image of God; and
> the root in the very heart of God Himself.[4]

In our modern setting, the use of natural law is substantially more problematic. Contemporary culture is geared toward preference, which is a far cry even from natural law. That being the case, Christians have a much more difficult time building an apologetic case for a particular ethical issue. Why wouldn't or shouldn't Christians use the authoritative Word to present God's case to the culture? John Frame puts it into perspective when he writes, "There is no reason to deprive unbelieving society of this authoritative source, when they need it so badly, and when they need to know so much that natural law cannot supply."[5]

At the same time, natural law was viewed as a complement to what Scripture taught. Both Luther and Calvin certainly had their detractors, however. In 1764, over 100 years later, an Italian lawyer named Cesare Beccaria challenged Calvin's views in a work entitled *On Crimes and Punishments* and in other writings. One of the earliest pleas for the abolition of capital punishment, Beccaria's work was quite influential in its time, especially in England. What were Beccaria's arguments? Without going into all of them, he plainly believed that there had been a useless profusion of punishments that, to his mind, "never made men better." Beccaria, apparently not considering what God's Word taught, asked,

> What *right*...have men to cut the throats of their fellow-
> creatures? Did any one ever give to others the right
> of taking away his life? If it were so, how shall it be
> reconciled to the maxim that tells us that a man has
> no right to kill himself?

Furthermore, Beccaria was convinced that "the punishment of death is not authorized by any right...." Beccaria likened the death penalty to "a war of a whole nation against a citizen." He did concede, however, that the general public considered capital punishment "useful to the general good."[6]

There were legitimate reasons for some of Beccaria's comments, questions, and objections. England was in dire need of reform regarding the use of capital punishment. Two examples come to mind. In 1814, three young English boys were executed for stealing a pair of shoes! And, in 1833, a nine-year-old boy was hanged for stealing a set of children's paints – paints, not pants! – from a London store. With such shocking excesses taking place, it is no wonder that Beccaria's work increased sympathy in England for the abolition of capital punishment. Even today, opponents of capital punishment use his writings as authoritative resources.

Capital punishment was first carried out in the United States in 1622 in the colony of Virginia. A man named Daniel Frank was hanged for stealing a calf and other items from Sir George Yeardley. In 1630, in Plymouth, Massachusetts, John Billington was the first person hanged for murder. John Jefferson (Jack) Davis, D.D., Professor of Systematic Theology, notes that,

> During the revolutionary period, most of the colonies considered murder, treason, piracy, arson, rape, robbery, burglary, and sodomy to be capital crimes. Hanging was the usual form of execution.[7]

During the eighteenth and nineteenth centuries, a number of influential people – men like Voltaire, Rousseau, Marx, Hume, Bentham, Franklin, and Paine – protested against the death penalty. The nineteenth century, with its romanticism and more liberal attitudes, was a period when opposition to the death penalty increased. By the middle 1900s, the American Society for the Abolition of Capital Punishment was founded and at least three states had abandoned capital punishment for all crimes except treason; other states soon followed suit. However, not all those states continued in this direction for "at one time or another, at least twenty-three states abolished the death penalty and at least twelve restored the penalty after having rescinded it."[8]

The largest number of judicial executions in the United States occurred from 1930–49, an average of 148 per year. Only a little more than a decade later, in the early 1960s, all that changed. America entered into a period of unprecedented unrest, social outrage, and near anarchy against various levels of the "Establishment" and "Military Industrial Complex." As part of the subculture moved farther and farther away from traditional values and appreciation of and for the history of the country, ethical tolerance grew. It was, indeed, the time to make love and not war. It was in vogue to question each and every authority. As a result, societal, political, and moral views changed considerably – exponentially – and that for the worst. Capitalism was "out" and socialism and communism were "in." Sexual promiscuity, pornography, and drug abuse also became more common and rampant. During that turbulent decade, in 1967, *without any significant legislative action*, the use of the death penalty came to a halt.[9] This lack of legislative action would become one of the harbingers of things to come.*

On June 29, 1972, however, the Supreme Court of the United States handed down a monumental ruling concerning capital punishment. In *Furman v. Georgia*, the court ruled – by a 5 to 4 split decision – that the imposition of the death penalty in the states of Texas and Georgia violated both the Eighth and Fourteenth Amendments to the U.S. Constitution.† Paul D. and John

---

* For example, in 1983, at the tenth anniversary of *Roe v. Wade*, President Reagan wrote a long article entitled "Abortion and the Conscience of the Nation," and in it, said this: "Our nationwide policy of abortion-on-demand through all nine months of pregnancy was neither voted for by our people nor enacted by our legislators – not a single state had such unrestricted abortion before the Supreme Court decreed it to be national policy in 1973.... Make no mistake, abortion-on-demand is not a right granted by the Constitution." (See Davis, 15-16.)

† The Eighth Amendment forbids cruel and unusual punishments. The Fourteenth Amendment requires equal protection under the law.

S. Feinberg (evangelical theologians), comment that "Prior to 1972 some 5,707 people were legally executed for capital crimes in the U.S.," pointing to the truth since the death penalty was not used indiscriminately, it was considered a viable means of punishment up to the beginning of the 1970s. In response to this decision, thirty-five states began to rewrite their capital punishment laws so they would conform to the Supreme Court's ruling in *Furman v. Georgia*. It was not until July 2, 1976, by a 7 to 2 margin, that the Court declared most of the new statutes acceptable. After four years, the death penalty was legal again. In 1977, executions resumed."[10] That was the year Gary Gilmore died before a Utah firing squad. Today, in many states, capital punishment is still legal. In some states like California, however, it is rarely implemented and convicted murderers die more often from old age and suicide than they do from actually being executed.

Before the Supreme Court reinstated the death penalty, many past detractors of the death penalty predicted that the United States would be subject to a veritable blood bath and executions would be an almost daily occurrence. That did not occur; they were greatly mistaken. In fact, the opposite has been the case. Death row prisoners are "seldom executed in the U.S., and only after a lengthy appeal process in the courts. As a result, the numbers on death row continue to grow."[11] Economist John R. Lott, Jr. makes a comment that is very applicable here: "If something becomes more costly, people will do less of it. This is the fundamental principle of economics – a simple notion that also explains a lot of human behavior in realms seemingly far removed from trade, industry, and finance."[12]* This argument will recur when we deal with the notion of deterrence.

---

* In *Freedomnomics*, "Parting Shots," Lott says similarly: "Adam Smith had it right: individuals, by pursuing their own self-interest, enrich society. Smith understood the fundamental principle of economics: when you make something more costly, people will do less of it. *In other words, incentives matter.*" (Lott, 193. *Emphasis added.*)

3

THE DEATH PENALTY
IN CHURCH HISTORY

L ET us now delve a little more deeply into how the church
has thought about this ethical issue. Within the church, just
as in secular society, opinions about capital punishment have
varied and still vary. Among the early church fathers, Lucius
Lactantius (ca. A.D. 240–320) opposed the death penalty, while
St. Augustine (A.D. 354–430) spoke in favor of the state's right
to impose it. During the Middle Ages, when executions were
extremely cruel and torture before death was common, church-
men had raging debates about the appropriateness of capital
punishment. Even so, one of the greatest theologians of that age,
St. Thomas Aquinas (1224/25–1274), argued for the right of the
state to impose capital punishment for certain crimes.[1]

We briefly alluded earlier to the fact that John Calvin was
a proponent of capital punishment in certain situations. Here,
I want to flesh out those comments by referencing both his
Institutes as well as his commentary on the book of Romans.
Calvin discusses capital punishment and its compatibility with
Christian piety in his *Institutes of the Christian Religion* (4.20.10).

After reminding the reader that the civil magistrate is ordained by God, Calvin asks this question:

> If the law of God forbids all Christians to kill [Exod. 20:13; Deut. 5:17; Matt. 5:21], and the prophet prophesies concerning God's holy mountain (the church) that in it men shall not afflict or hurt [Isa. 11:9; 65:25] – how can magistrates be pious men and shedders of blood at the same time?

He answers his question with these words:

> ...if we understand that the magistrate in administering punishments does nothing by himself, but carries out the very judgments of God, we shall not be hampered by this scruple. The law of the Lord forbids killing; but, that murderers may not go unpunished, the Lawgiver himself puts into the hand of his ministers a sword to be drawn against all murderers.

Calvin presses this Biblical claim of the death penalty further when he says:

> They do not bear the sword in vain, says Paul, for they are ministers of God to execute His wrath, avengers of wrongdoers [Rom. 13:4]. Therefore, if princes and other rulers recognize that nothing is more acceptable to the Lord than their obedience, let them apply themselves to this ministry, if, indeed, they are intent on having their piety, righteousness, and uprightness approved of God [cf. II Tim. 2:15].[2]

He follows a similar line of reasoning in his commentary on the book of Romans. Calvin sets the stage in his comments on 13:4 this way:

> Magistrates may hence learn what their vocation is, for they are not to rule for their own interest, but for

the public good; nor are they endued with unbridled power, but what is restricted to the wellbeing of their subjects; in short, they are responsible to God and to men in the exercise of their power.

When the matter of the state bearing the sword is addressed, Calvin gives us these comments:

> It is another part of the office of magistrates, that they ought *forcibly* to repress the waywardness of evil men, who do not willingly suffer themselves to be governed by laws, and *to inflict such a punishment on their offences as God's judgment requires*; for He expressly declares, that they are armed with the sword, not for an empty show, but that they may *smite* evil-doers.[3]

Then, in order to insure that there is no misunderstanding about what he is saying, Calvin summarizes his thoughts this way:

> This is a remarkable passage for the purpose of proving the right of the sword; for if the Lord, by arming the magistrate, has also committed to him the use of the sword, *whenever he visits the guilty with death*, by executing God's vengeance, he obeys His commands. *Contend then do they with God who think it unlawful to shed the blood of wicked men.*[4]

Opponents of capital punishment in the Christian church today often ask this same question about how our governing authorities can be shedders of blood. However, Calvin's answer, written in 1559, has not lost either its clarity or power. It is still as true today as it was in the sixteenth century. Yet, because the world today has no stomach for the God of Scripture or the serious mention of His Name in public, fewer people accept that the state actually does carry out God's judgments. Some have come to believe that freedom *of* religion means freedom *from* religion. Separation of church and state now seems to mean the separation of God *from* the state for some liberal-leaning Christians as well as secularists.

The Bible also rejects absolute church/state separation because God is the ruler of all of life, not just the spiritual side of life. God created the state, and the magistrate derives his authority from Him. Another way of saying it is this: God is sovereign over all human states, even when they try to separate from Him and His authority. The state derives its legitimate authority from God. Using Biblical texts such as Proverbs 17:15* and Proverbs 20:26,† Calvin then adds a powerful warning:

> Would that this was ever before our minds – that nothing is done here *from men's rashness,* but all things are done *on the authority of God who commands it;* and while His authority goes before us, we never wander from the straight path![5]

Calvin also warns those who execute justice and have the power to sentence a criminal to death to guard their attitudes:

> I am not one either to favor *undue cruelty* or think that a fair judgment can be pronounced unless clemency, that best counselor of kings and surest keeper of the kingly throne (as Solomon declares) [Prov. 20:28] is always present – clemency, which by a certain writer of antiquity was truly called the chief gift of princes.[6]

By comparing what Calvin means by the word "clemency" with his other writings, it is obvious that Calvin is not opting for releasing the convicted felon, neither is he asserting that the state should show mercy. He is arguing, rather, for what he

---

* He who justifies the wicked and he who condemns the righteous are both alike an abomination to the LORD.

† A wise king winnows the wicked and drives the wheel over them.

had just stated: no undue cruelty and for fair judgment. Then he wisely adds,

> Yet it is necessary for the magistrate to pay attention to both, lest by excessive severity he either harm more than heal; or, by *superstitious affection of clemency*, fall into *the cruelest gentleness*, if he should (with a soft and dissolute kindness) abandon many to their destruction...*it is indeed bad to live under a prince with whom nothing is permitted; but much worse under one by whom everything is allowed.*[7]

Calvin's balanced position of no undue cruelty and fair judgment is foundational and represents a clear and ageless Biblical viewpoint. Thankfully, it is still the position of many Christians today.

What Do the Westminster Standards Say?

In addition to the view of a number of great theologians, it is also quite interesting to read what the confessions of the church have to say about the law of God, the standards God gives us, and their application in our lives. Reformed Biblical (or covenant) theology emphasizes that there is an overarching line of continuity between the Old and New Testaments (excellently explained by Calvin[8]), all the while recognizing that there are areas of discontinuity as well.

For example, the dietary laws and what we typically call the ceremonial or sacrificial laws have been abrogated by the coming of the promised Messiah in the New Testament. On the other hand, the Old Testament sacraments of circumcision and Passover have been modified into Baptism and the Lord's Supper.

Regarding morals, throughout the entire Bible God gives us laws and standards for the ethical behavior of His people. Greg Bahnsen, PH.D., the late professor of ethics, gives us a useful interpretive principle: Unless the New Testament clearly alters or abrogates something in the Old Testament, those Old Testament laws are still in effect.[9]

Regarding salvation, Abrahamic faith and God's covenant of grace with Israel in the Old Testament are also found in the New Testament. Both testaments teach *one means of salvation* and the existence of *one people of God.* Old Testament Israelites were not saved by the keeping of the law nor are New Testament believers. Abraham's *faith,* not his works, was counted to him as righteousness (cf. Gen. 15:6; Rom. 4:1-25).

We contend, therefore, that in God there is but *one* standard of measure for all history, for the Old *and* New Testament eras. Furthermore, this single standard applies to both believer and nonbeliever. One clear example will suffice. When God destroyed Sodom and Gomorrah for its wickedness, He did not use a different standard of righteousness than He used for His people.

As Frame tells us, accepting the Bible as a whole is especially important for Christians to do, as servants of the Lord Jesus Christ, who have His commandments and keep them (cf. John 14:15, 21, 23; 15:10; 1 John 2:3-5; 3:21-24; 5:3). It is also true that everything in the Bible is ethical in this sense: "Even when Scripture expounds doctrinal propositions, it presents them as propositions that *ought* to be believed." This is true for both Christians and non-Christians; for both the Old as well as the New Testament. In other words, all ethics is religious, even when it tries to be secular. In the end, all ethics presupposes ultimate values.

Simultaneously,

> Ethics is theology, viewed as a means of determining which persons, acts, and attitudes receive God's blessing and which do not.[10]

While the nonbeliever *may* thumb his nose and scoff at such language, the serious believer must take these admonitions seriously and make a study of the proper Biblical interpretation of the truth found in God's revealed will.

Three Types of Law in the Old Testament

Having said that, let's take a moment and listen to what the Westminster Standards say about the various laws and their application to the New Testament Church. In chapter 19 of the Westminster Confessional Standards under the heading "The Law of God," we find an explanation of the three types of law found in the Old Testament:

CEREMONIAL Law—

> God was pleased to give to the people of Israel, as a Church under age, *ceremonial laws*, containing several typical ordinances, partly for worship, prefiguring Christ, his graces, actions, sufferings, and benefits; and partly to hold forth diverse instructions of moral duties. *All which ceremonial laws are now abrogated under the New Testament.*

JUDICIAL LAW—

> The Standards continue: "To them also, as a body politic, he gave *sundry judicial laws, which expired together with the State of that people....*"

Not all of these categories are as clear cut as we often think. Nevertheless, this is not a hopeless quagmire, where no answers whatsoever are to be found. Two examples will suffice here. First, Deuteronomy 4:5-6 states that God taught His people statutes and rules. The explicit command is:

> Keep them and do them, for that will be your wisdom and your understanding in the sight *of the peoples....* (*Emphasis added.*)

19

In Matthew's Gospel (5:17-20), these words are recorded as coming from the mouth of our Lord:

> Do not think that I have come to abolish the Law or the Prophets; I have not come to abolish them but to fulfill them. For truly, I say to you, until heaven and earth pass away, not an iota, not a dot, will pass from the Law until all is accomplished. Therefore whoever relaxes one of the least of these commandments and teaches others to do the same will be called least in the kingdom of heaven, but whoever does them and teaches them will be called great in the kingdom of heaven.

Clearly – because He says it twice – Jesus did not come to abolish the Law of God, but to fulfill it. Whatever nuance you place on the word "fulfill," it cannot mean "abolish," since Jesus reiterated twice that He did not come to abolish the law.

The late Dutch New Testament scholar, Herman Ridderbos, wrote this about Jesus' words in Matthew 5:17:

> In the second half of verse 17, Jesus repeats that He has not come to abolish. Here, however, He adds the positive side of His work: He had come to fulfill the Law and the Prophets. The Greek word translated "fulfill" literally means to give a vessel that is completely or partially empty its appropriate content. To fulfill the law thus means to ensure that it receives the full obedience that is its due, to bring fully to light its true and deepest meaning.[11]

THE MORAL LAW –

The moral law, the third type spoken of in the Standards, is very different in one special way from the other two,

> *The moral law binds all forever*, justified persons as well as others, to the obedience thereof;...in regard to the matter contained in it but also in respect of the authority of God the Creator, who gave it. Neither does Christ, in

the Gospel, any way dissolve, but must strengthen this obligation. (Westminster Confession of Faith, 19.5. *Italics added.*)

The moral law was the only type of law that did not expire nor was it abrogated. Instead it binds all forever by God's standards of judgment. Nevertheless, this interpretive tool must be applied judiciously and wisely. For example, the Ten Commandments are surely the most obvious candidate for what constitutes the "moral law." By studying the Ten Commandments in their literal and spiritual senses as well as in their prohibitions and affirmations, the Christian is given absolute moral guidance regarding how he is to live a life that is pleasing to the Lord; that is in accordance with God's revealed will.

Dr. Lee demonstrates the centrality of the Ten Commandments in this manner:

> Christ's teachings include a strong emphasis on keeping the whole Decalogue. For they are thoroughly consistent with the essential righteousness of His Own Law-Abiding Person.[12]

What should we take away from this brief discussion? Jack Davis summarizes thus:

> The abrogation of the specifics of the Mosaic covenant (e.g., circumcision, dietary laws, animal sacrifice) for the New Testament Church *does not necessarily affect the moral and legal principles given through Noah.*[13]

This is because Christ Himself fulfilled those prophetic aspects of the Law. Explicitly, this would include continuation of the "life-for-life" requirement in Genesis 9:6.

Examining the Biblical Principles

Christians are obligated to conform their thinking and actions to the Word of God. It is important that they do not neglect to

study and meditate upon God's Word. They must not let emotions form their principles but must allow the Word of God to
determine their principles. We are now ready to examine the
pertinent texts on the relevant foundational Scriptures dealing
directly and indirectly with capital punishment.

4

FROM THE

OLD TESTAMENT

IN the Old Testament, the following offenses were considered capital crimes: murder, the smiting or striking of one's father or mother, kidnapping, cursing of one's father or mother, witchcraft, bestiality, idolatry, prostitution, blasphemy, cursing the LORD, Sabbath violation, enticing to idolatry, being a false prophet, adultery, rape, and perjury (cf. Exod. 21:12-17; Lev. 20:9; Prov. 20:20; Matt. 15:4; Mark 7:10; Deut. 24:7; Exod. 22:18; Exod. 22:19; Lev. 20:15-16; Deut. 17:2-5; Lev. 24:16; Exod. 31:14; Deut. 13:6-10; Deut: 13:1-5; Deut. 22:22; Deut. 22:25).[1] John Frame adds incest (Lev. 20:11-14), sodomy (Lev. 18:22; 20:13), false witness in capital crimes (Deut. 19:16-20), fornication by a priest's daughter (Lev. 21:9), human sacrifice (Lev. 20:2-5), incorrigible juvenile delinquents (Deut. 21:18-21), sacrificing to false gods (Exod. 22:20), and contempt for the priest or the judge (Deut. 17:12) to the list.[2] Although to our modern or postmodern minds, some of these crimes seem antiquated and out of touch with our contemporary situation, we have much to learn from Scripture. What I mean here is this: Christians and everyone must be prepared to bow before the absolute authority of God's Word as well as submit to God's lordship in our lives. Part of gospel obedience is recognizing and applying the truth that God is good and does only good, even if we don't understand it (cf. Ps. 119:68). God is good even when He manifests His goodness mysteriously. Moreover, our modern mind and mindset is not the measure by which we should determine truth from falsehood. When we turn to Scripture, we are reminded that what might seem harsh to us actually is not. The author of the letter to the Hebrews states that in the Old Testament "every transgression or disobedience received a just penalty" (Heb. 2:2). It is not as if the Lord was depopulating the earth; He was, rather, purging the evil from its midst (cf. Deut. 13:5; 17:7, 12; 19:19; 21:21; 22:21-22, 24; 24:7; Judg. 20:13). Simultaneously, we must also keep in mind what we've already learned from chapter nineteen of the Westminster Confession of Faith.

Capital Punishment and Man Created in the Image of God (Genesis 9:5-6).

"The theological background of 'You shall not murder' is that God is the Lord of life," according to Frame.[3] One of the finest texts to explain this point is found in the first book of Moses. Genesis 9:5-6 is a foundational text in our consideration of the question of capital punishment.[4] Walter Kaiser, Old Testament Professor, believes that

> The life of an individual made in the image of God was so valued that all violent forms of snatching life away had to be requited on God's terms, not on human terms.[5]

W. S. Bruce, Minister of Banff, Edinburgh, in his comments about this topic, asserted that the word "that guards the sanctity of God's best gift, makes murder the greatest crime that man can

4 FROM THE OLD TESTAMENT

perpetrate against his fellow."[6] In order to understand clearly what Scripture teaches us here, we must carefully examine the covenant God made with Noah after the flood when the Lord God said to Noah,

> And for your lifeblood I will require a reckoning: from every beast I will require it and from man. From his fellow man I will require a reckoning for the life of man. "Whoever sheds the blood of man, by man shall his blood be shed; for God made man in His own image." (vv. 5-6).

Following what we've previously learned, this commandment to Noah was nowhere abrogated or altered by New Testament teaching. Therefore let us discover why the nature of this covenant is so central in our understanding of the death penalty. The late Professor of Systematic Theology, John Murray, gives us four helpful guidelines.

The FIRST thing that must be realized about God's covenant with Noah is that it was "conceived, devised, determined, established, confirmed, and dispensed by God Himself." In other words, it was *unilateral*, which means that no action was required of Noah. God *sovereignly* imposed it. God did not ask for human permission, cooperation, or approval to make this covenant. He simply declared His will and did it, according to His divine freedom and good pleasure.

SECOND, it is a *universal* covenant. It applied to Noah, his seed, every living creature on earth, and included inanimate flood waters (vv. 9–11). It is a covenant of blessing containing a promise by God "to all flesh, even those people who are wholly unaware of its existence." As was stated above, God is revealed to us as a good God. Part of His goodness manifests itself in the removal of every murderer. The all-inclusive Noahic covenant is meant to have universal application, which extends to the pronouncement of the lawful, God-ordained execution of murderers.

THIRD, the covenant with Noah is also *unconditional*. Human unfaithfulness will not and cannot nullify it. No matter what man does, God will always keep what He promised to Noah. The rainbow is God's constant reminder that He will be faithful to His promise.

FOURTH, God's covenant with Noah "is an *everlasting* covenant" (vv. 12, 16).[7] It is wholly divine in its beginning, its fulfillment, and its confirmation; it will have no earthly end. This is why we must believe that the words God spoke to Noah do apply in today's world. All of these points are closely connected to God's requirement of "a reckoning for the life of man" for all ages and times.

In other words, as Calvin said, God "accounts the life of men precious."[8] Old Testament scholar Claus Westermann teaches that Genesis 9:5-6 clearly speaks about the prohibition of shedding man's blood by either a beast or man. Both are held accountable for taking a man's life. Beasts that kill men must be put to death.[9] More importantly, God requires an accounting from each man for the life of his fellow man. Herein, God places "in the hand of man His own judicial power." Martin Luther believed that Genesis 9:5-6 lays the foundation for divinely appointed civil magistrates who are to execute judicial rights when a man's life is taken (cf. Matt. 23:35).[10]

Not only does Genesis 9 give us a foundation for civil government; it also gives us a reason why murder is a capital crime. Murder is a capital crime because man is made in the image of God. Being God's image bearer gives man a particular value that can never be eradicated. Calvin adds this:

> Men are indeed unworthy of God's care...but since they bear the image of God engraved on them, God deems Himself violated in their person.[11]

Man's value is *God-given* and *God-ordained.* God's continued gracious dealings with man means that,

> although they have nothing of their own by which they obtain the favor of God, He looks upon His own gifts in them, and is thereby excited to love and to care for them.[12]

Here we see the clear language of the sanctity of human life: *"Man's divine creation should be a deterrent to criminal behavior."*[13] What Victor P. Hamilton, religion professor, Asbury College, means to say here is that since man is created in the image of God, that, in and of itself, should be an adequate deterrent. In theory, of course, he is correct. The problem arises in society when murderers will not acknowledge the truth of the *imago.* Hamilton's thesis is a common one in Christian circles: Murder is punished with death because to kill another human being is to destroy one who is a bearer of the divine image. However,

> it is evident that the infliction of the punishment was not to be left to the caprice of individuals, but belonged to those alone who represent the authority and majesty of God, i.e., the divinely appointed rulers, who for that very reason are called *Elohim** in Ps. 82:6.[14]

In light of the universal character of the Noahic covenant and the New Testament emphasis on the right of civil magistrates to execute convicted murderers, Hamilton's assertions have a twofold application: First, they direct us to the inherent value that every human being has due to the fact that he is created in the image of God. Second, by extension into the New Testament epoch, there is the abiding principle for the civil magistrate to execute the death penalty upon those who struck at God by the

---

* The Hebrew word *Elohim* means, among other things, "gods." In Psalm 82:6, which Jesus quotes in John 10:35, it is used of the judges of Israel.

murder of one created in His image *and* to purge the evil from the midst of the land.

Whenever the value of human life is downplayed and denigrated, as it is so often in our modern society, the value of human beings depreciates. When we make little of striking down the image bearer, we reveal a terrifying lack of understanding of the holiness and worth of the Image-Giver. Calvin explains it this way:

> …no one can be injurious to his brother without wounding God himself. Were this doctrine deeply fixed in our minds, we should be much more reluctant than we are to inflict injuries.[15]

Therefore, God's command in Genesis 9:5-6 lays the foundation for all civil government and forms an unalterable command to protect the life of man as well as to punish the perpetrator of the crime of murder.

> The murderer is to suffer that which he has inflicted; for murder is not only the extreme of unbrotherliness, but also a crime against the inviolable majesty of the Divine image, which even after the Fall is fundamentally the *character indelebilis* of mankind and of each individual.[16]

After the Flood, God made a promise that He was bound by His holiness, truthfulness, and faithfulness to keep. If God ceased to bring exterminating judgment upon earthly creations, then it was necessary for Him, by His commands and authority, to erect a barrier against the supremacy of evil, and thus lay the foundation for a well-ordered civil development of humanity, in accordance with the words of His blessing (to Noah).[17] It is unfortunate that our society is not willing to listen to this noteworthy divine truth. We shall now listen to what the sixth commandment teaches us on this subject.

The Sixth Commandment: Murder versus Killing

> What the sixth commandment basically says is that life and death are God's business. He is Lord of life and death, and we may not take life without His authorization.[18]

Without getting too technical, I do want to take a moment and explain the use of the Hebrew word in Exodus 20:13. According to the *Theological Wordbook of the Old Testament*,

> *Rāṣaḥ* is a purely Hebrew term. It has no clear cognate in any of the contemporary tongues. The root occurs thirty-eight times in the Old Testament, with fourteen occurrences in Numbers 35. The initial use of the root appears in the Ten Commandments (Exod. 20:13). In that important text it appears in the simple Qal stem with the negative adverb, "You shall not murder."[19]

It is essential to make this point at the outset because many today – even in the Christian community – desire to circumvent the clear teaching of Scripture.[20]

Simultaneously, it is patently true that the sixth commandment describes more than premeditated murder. This appears in the broader meaning of the word used in Exodus 20:13 and especially in Numbers 35. "The many occurrences in Numbers 35 deal with the organization of the six cities of refuge to which manslayers who accidentally killed a person could flee. Numbers 35:11 makes completely clear that the refuge was for those guilty of unpremeditated, accidental killings. This makes clear that *rāṣaḥ* applies equally to cases of both premeditated murder and killings as a result of any other circumstances, what English

Common Law has called "manslaughter." In passing it should also be noted that *rāṣaḥ* describes killing for revenge (Num. 35:27, 30) and assassination (2 Kings 6:32).[21]

The Hebrew verb *ratsakh* or *rāṣaḥ* admittedly has a broader application than murder. Quite often, it can also refer

> to killing that is unlawful or forbidden. It is not used for the killing of animals or for killing in war. That would suggest that the best translation here is 'murder,' not the more general 'kill.' However, the term differs from our English word *murder* in that it applies to manslaughter and negligent homicide.[22]

The so-called "manslaughter" texts, for example, get us deeper into the theological and ethical implications of the sixth commandment and the cities of refuge in the Old Testament (cf. Exod. 21:12-14; Num. 35:9-34; Deut. 19:1-13; Josh. 20:1-9), and would take us rather far afield of the subject of the book. What is particularly instructive about these texts and the "cities of refuge," however, is that even if the killing were unintentional, the concept of the image of God in man is so crucial and central that the one who committed manslaughter had to flee to a city of refuge and remain there until the death of the high priest (cf. Num. 35:26-28).

That is to say, even the *un*intentional taking of life is protected in a certain sense, and God's justice requires a severe reckoning for the deed.

Christians who assert that the sixth commandment prohibits *all* killing or, even more specifically, that it somehow prohibits the death penalty, have sorely missed the Biblical point. What the sixth commandment does is to prohibit individuals from taking the law into their own hands and killing for hate, for gain, or for getting even or trying to square wrongs on their own. However, the sixth commandment in no way prohibits states from bringing murderers to justice through capital punishment.

One of the most comprehensive explanations of the duties required by the sixth commandment is found in the Westminster Larger Catechism (Q/A 135-136):

What are the duties required in the sixth commandment?
 The duties required in the sixth commandment are, all careful studies, and lawful endeavors, *to preserve the life of ourselves and others* by resisting all thoughts and purposes, subduing all passions, and *avoiding all occasions, temptations, and practices, which tend to the unjust taking away the life of any; but just defense thereof against violence,* patient bearing of the hand of God, quietness of mind, cheerfulness of spirit; a sober use of meat, drink, physical sleep, labor, and recreations; by charitable thoughts, love, compassion, meekness, gentleness, kindness; peaceable, mild and courteous speeches and behavior; forbearance, readiness to be reconciled, patient bearing and forgiving of injuries, and requiting good for evil; comforting and succoring the distressed, *and protecting and defending the innocent. (Emphasis added.)**

Thereafter, we find what is forbidden:
 What are the sins forbidden in the sixth commandment?

 The sins forbidden in the sixth commandment are, all taking away the life of ourselves, or of others, *except in case of public justice, lawful war, or necessary defense;* the neglecting or withdrawing the lawful and necessary means of preservation of life; sinful anger, hatred, envy, desire of revenge; all excessive passions, distracting cares; immoderate use of meat, drink, labor, and recreations; provoking words, oppression, quarreling,

---

* See Eph. 5:28-29; 1 Kings 18:4; Jer. 26:15-16; Acts 23:12, 16-17, 21, 27; Eph. 4:26-27; Ps. 82:4; Prov. 24:11-12; James 5:7-11.

striking, wounding, and whatsoever else tends to the destruction of the life of any. (*Emphasis added.*)*

In the Heidelberg Catechism (Lord's Day 40, Q/A 105-106) we find the following list of requirements for the sixth commandment:

> I am not to dishonor, hate, injure, or kill my neighbor by thoughts, words, or gestures, and much less by deeds, whether personally or through another; rather, I am to put away all desire of revenge. Moreover, I am not to harm or recklessly endanger myself. Therefore, also, the government bears the sword to prevent murder.†

The Heidelberg continues by adding certain *attitudinal* requirements as well:

> By forbidding murder, God teaches us that He hates the root of murder, such as envy, hatred, anger, and desire of revenge, and that He regards all these as murder. When God condemns envy, hatred, and anger, He commands us to love our neighbor as ourselves, to show patience, peace, gentleness, mercy, and friendliness toward him, to protect him from harm as much as we can, and to do good even to our enemies.‡

Notice the strong teaching about the *spiritual* nature of the sixth commandment in both catechisms. Since all of life is ethical, Christians must remember in their discussions about capital punishment that the Christian's ultimate goal is to worship and glorify God by living life on God's terms only. Real health for mankind is spiritual wholeness based on God's Law.

---

* See Acts 16:28; Num. 35:31,33; Jer. 48:10; Exod. 22:2-3; Matt. 25:42; Eph. 4:31.

† Compare Gen. 9:6; Lev. 19:17-18; Matt. 5:21-22; 26:52; Prov. 25:21-22; Matt. 18:35; Rom. 12:19; Eph. 4:26; Matt. 4:7; Rom. 13:11-14; Exod. 21:14; Rom. 13:4.

‡ Compare Prov. 14:30; Rom. 1:29; Rom. 12:10,18,19,20; Gal. 5:19-21; James 1:20; 1 John 2:9-11; 3:15; Matt. 7:12; 22:39; Matt. 5:5; Luke 6:36; Gal. 6:1-2; Eph. 4:2; Col. 3:12; 1 Pet. 3:8; Exod. 23:4-5; Matt. 5:44-45.

In summary, the sixth commandment requires us to see human beings as those whose image-bearing nature gives them inherent value. It prohibits unlawful death by premeditated means such as murder, abortion, suicide, reckless self-endangerment, or any harm because of envy, hatred, anger, and revenge. It allows the killing or execution of criminals by lawful means, legitimate lethal force by law enforcement, and just wars in which enemies from an aggressor nation are killed by the armed forces. In addition, individuals may defend themselves or protect the defenseless as well, in the absence of ordained authority. This is entirely in keeping with Christian principles. It is an established fact in the United States that the courts have found no obligation on the part of law enforcement departments to protect individuals.[23] When you stop and think about that, it becomes apparent that it is a virtual impossibility. Each citizen would have to have law enforcement accessible personally 24/7. Most municipalities have written into their by-laws that law enforcement is immune from the obligation for individual protection of citizens.

The Divine Reason for the Death Penalty: To Purge the Evil from Our Midst

The command to purge evil from the community of God's people by judicially executing evildoers is found in nine Old Testament passages.* The Hebrew word for "purge," *bâʿar,* carries with it the notion of burning out, purging by fire. It is through the presence of a severe and frightening penalty that the seriousness of this commandment is revealed. When an opponent of capital punishment claims that *it does not deter*

---

* False prophecy, Deut. 13:5. Putting away the guilt of innocent blood, Deut. 13:13. Witnesses first in executing stoning, Deut. 17:7. Showing contempt for judges and priests, Deut. 17:12. False witness, Deut. 19:16-19. Rebellion against parents, Deut. 21:18-21. Fornication, Deut. 22:21, 22, 24. Kidnapping, Deut. 24:7. Rape and murder, Judges 20:13.

murder, we must realize that our opponent is actually guessing. No one really knows how many would-be murderers have controlled murderous urges because the death penalty is in effect. It is difficult to catalogue "possible" murders since no one can read minds but God. Nevertheless, for a Christian, the words of Proverbs 21:15-16 certainly seem to say that justice actively pursued can be a significant deterrent to crime.* There are specific Biblical guidelines as to how *precisely* the evil is to be purged.

First, *the purging of evil must be just.* Justice is a key theme in the Bible. For example, in Deuteronomy 16:20, we read:

> Justice, and only justice, you shall follow, that you may live and inherit the land that the LORD your God is giving you.

Justice is necessary for society to function well. Under divine directives from God, the people and the magistrates in the ancient Israel theocracy were to pursue justice and justice alone. Today, we are to do the same. In both the legislation of laws as well as in the punishments of law breakers, justice should prevail.

Second, *the perversion of justice must be disdained.*

> The pursuit of justice alone provided a basis for the execution of the law that was not merely human, whereas perverting justice reduced the execution of the law to a human basis in which unjust criteria became operative.[24]

In the Old Testament, the method of execution was usually death by stoning (cf. Lev. 20:2; 24:16; Num. 15:35; Deut. 13:10; 17:5; 21:21; 22:21; 22:24). Deuteronomy 17:5-7 lays out the ground rules for establishing guilt and the punishment. First, two or three eyewitnesses had to testify; only one person testifying was not

---

* When justice is done, it is a joy to the righteous but terror to evildoers. One who wanders from the way of good sense will rest in the assembly of the dead.

enough. Then, the witnesses themselves were to cast the first stones, and afterwards all the people would join in the act of judgment. Peter C. Craigie, late Dean of Humanities, University of Calgary, and author of many works on Old Testament and Ugaritic languages, points out that,

> the way in which the execution was to be carried out emphasizes the burden of responsibility for *truthful* testimony that rested on the witness in a case involving capital punishment. [Although] the execution was to be carried out *communally*, in the first instance, the hand of the *witness* shall be against him. [Finally,] having given true evidence, the witness cast the first stones, but shared the responsibility with the whole community. Thus, all together would completely remove the evil. The capital punishment of the offender removed that evil which had, by the nature of the crime, endangered the continuation of the covenant community of God.[25]

Today, many citizens are disillusioned and have become cynical about the entire judicial system, not just the death penalty. They watch in dismay as criminals, through legal wrangling, plea bargains, nonsensical technicalities, or legal errors escape the just punishment due their crime. Others embrace arguments for leniency based upon documented cases of accused people wrongfully convicted and wrongfully executed. In the process, the prison system seems to them to have become based more on pop psychology and politics than applied justice. Since our country has long since abandoned Biblical truth, it sees no measure of reasonableness in a text such as Ecclesiastes 8:11 that says,

> Because the sentence against an evil deed is not executed speedily, the heart of the children of man is fully set to do evil.

Deuteronomy 16:20 points to a concept that our nation needs to relearn: If God's people don't preserve justice, God won't preserve them in the land. Justice, the principle underlying the law, was not made or conceived by man but finds its source and authority in God. Therefore, God's justice is the *only* sure and authoritative basis for the law. The pursuit of justice and the just execution of the law lead to prosperity and life.[26] The purpose of applied justice, then, is not only the *punishment* of the evildoer but also the *preservation of the nation. It is not only to deter criminal behavior and crime.*

Allowing convicted murderers to live, to be given parole, to be released from prison, and, then, perhaps, to murder again, subjects our communities to a lack of protective preservation. Sadly, it is not unusual for another murder to take place by a convicted but released and "rehabilitated" murderer. Can you say recidivism? *Innocent blood* is shed because lawful justice was not applied.

Although modern men argue about whether or not capital punishment is an effective deterrent of crime, it is clear that God thinks it is. J. A. Thompson correctly notes that

> The threat of execution for such an offender (murderer) was designed to prevent the spread of infection and purge out the evil from the midst of Israel.[27]

Note that the command did not say that it would *totally* prevent the spread of others committing a similar crime. Nothing this side of paradise can or will be 100% effective. However, based upon the human experience of child raising, we must at least concede that *it may be possible* that strict punishment does prevent the spread of murder and other crimes. Good parents do not allow their children to play in busy streets. A child who understands that his parents will punish him severely if he plays in the street is less likely to play there. However, a child who knows his parents are lenient and tolerant of bad behavior will most likely go ahead and try playing in the busy street. Every good parent knows that punishment is a deterrent and every child knows that the anticipated level of punishment influences what he decides he will or will not do.

The Bible Requires Just Witnesses and True Testimony

Exodus 23:1-9 directs our attention to justice and how we are not to violate the rights of others. It informs us about the responsibilities and requirements of witnesses and judges in all cases. These verses allude to the Ten Commandments and remind us that we are not to spread false reports, be malicious witnesses, be one who perverts justice, be partial, take bribes, oppress a sojourner, or kill the innocent and righteous. A companion set of verses to the Exodus directives is found in Deuteronomy 19:15-21, where both the judges and witnesses are addressed. Reading these verses convinces us that

> There is a close association between the third and ninth commandment: the third prohibits swearing a false oath in the Lord's name (emphasizing a relationship between God and His people) and the ninth prohibits false witness between persons.[28]

Let's return to the Exodus 23 text for a moment. As we have seen in the Old Testament law code, the integrity of the witness was paramount. This is a far cry from some modern witnesses, who have few scruples about committing perjury because they have no fear of God. In the text under investigation, however, an Israelite was forbidden to be a "malicious witness" or a "witness of violence."* Someone who knowingly brings a false accusation or report against another person is such a witness.

---

* The NIV and NASB translate as "malicious" and the NKJV uses "unrighteous."

Such witnesses "join hands" with the wicked (v. 1). False reports pervert the justice of a bona fide legal system. They are both worthless and injurious and destroy the basic element of justice in a court of law.

Exodus 23 also teaches us about the *character* of a good witness. A witness could not side with the many or "fall in with the many." Following the crowd or siding with the majority to please men was not to be a witness's aim. His aim was to do justice. He could agree with the majority, but only when the majority opinion was just.

The teaching in this text reveals to us the injustice of making judgments and decisions based on our sympathies or preferences, especially when we are doing so in a court of law. However, because of the influence of political correctness in our modern society, there are plenty of excuses for bad behavior – poverty, background, race, or other such circumstances. The specific command here is to show neither favoritism nor partiality. What appears to be the reasoning behind this verse is the fuller explanation found in Leviticus 19:15:

> You shall do no injustice in court. You shall not be partial
> to the poor or defer to the great, but in righteousness
> shall you judge your neighbor.

From verses 4-5 of Exodus 23, we learn not to let even hatred for our enemy deter our impartiality, but to judge all men without partiality, dissension, or personal antipathy. In verse 9, we learn not to oppress the alien or sojourner. Because the Israelites had once been aliens in Egypt, they should have understood their vulnerabilities. They knew how it felt to live among people in a foreign society who had a different language and followed different customs. In the courts of Israel, aliens were supposed to receive justice and mercy similar to the native-born Israelites. Once again, we observe various layers in God's Word. In the midst of instruction regarding impartiality, we also find further directives embedded in the command regarding the application to aliens.

This text also addresses bribery, another pathway of injustice. When someone uses money, power, or position to manipulate honest witnesses and pervert justice, bribery occurs. It is a type of corruption that blinds those who are otherwise "clear-sighted" or discerning about a case. A nation cannot remain upright when bribery is present in its justice system. That is why bribery is such a serious sin. (cf. Exod. 18:21; 23:9; Deut. 10:17; 16:19; 27:25; Ps. 15:5; Prov. 17:23; Eccl. 7:7; Amos 5:12; Micah 3:11; 7:3.)

In Old Testament times, witnesses were governed by serious and extremely high standards. Partiality, bribery, and perjury were unacceptable. False testimony could cost a witness his or her life. In addition, there had to be at least two corroborating eyewitnesses or a person could not be found guilty. If, however, corroborating evidence proved guilt, appropriate punishment followed immediately.

The Bible Demands Both Mercy and Justice for All

The laws in the Old Testament provide principles of justice marked by consummate equity, impartiality, and gentleness. Exodus 22:21, 23:9 and Leviticus 19:33 exhort the Israelites not to oppress or exploit the foreigners among them. Leviticus 19:34 says,

> You shall treat the stranger who sojourns with you as the native among you, and you shall love him as yourself, for you were strangers in the land of Egypt: I am the LORD your God.

Further, Leviticus 24:22 states,

> You shall have the same rule for the sojourner and for
> the native, for I am the LORD your God."

Along similar lines, Deuteronomy 10:18 encourages justice for
all, tells the Israelites to care for orphans and widows, and to
love the foreigners among them.*

Consider also Leviticus 24 and Deuteronomy 19 in which God
explains that justice demands "an eye for an eye and a tooth
for a tooth." What is the Biblical principle here? For some, this
may sound like violent revenge. However, this commandment
is meant to prevent escalated and unjust retribution based on
personal vengeance and anger. The principle taught here is that
the severity of a punishment must fit the crime. That is undoubt-
edly a fair, just, and equitable expectation. In addition, God's
Word also teaches us about His righteousness. This is the chief
principle governing texts such as Obadiah 15, "As you have done,
it will be done to you; your deeds will return upon your own
head." This is a righteous and just judgment by God. The same
idea of God's character is found in texts like Jeremiah 50:29;
Habakkuk 2:8; Genesis 9:6; Revelation 16:6 and 18:6-7.

> God's judgments are fair in the most perfect way. In
> pleading for his nephew Lot, Abraham asks rhetorically,
> "Shall not the Judge of all the earth do what is just?"
> (Gen. 18:25).

Frame cites other texts that make the same point found in
Deuteronomy 32:4; Psalm 92:15; and Psalm 145:17. All this leads
to the conclusion regarding God's righteousness and justice that

> *All his judgments are righteous* (Ps. 9:8; 50:4-6; 51:4;
> 96:10, 13; 98:8-9), as in His law, the standard by which
> His judgments are made (Deut. 4:8; Ps. 19:7-9; 119:138, 142;
> Isa. 42:21). The fact that He judges all things in heaven

---

* See also Numbers 15:15-16, 29, which describe Israelites and foreigners subject to the
same laws.

and on earth implies that His standards are the highest standards of righteousness.[29]

Simultaneously, the gentleness of Old Testament law is demonstrated in Deuteronomy 22:6. There we read:

> If you come across a bird's nest in any tree or on the ground, with young ones or eggs and the mother sitting on the young or on the eggs, you shall not take the mother with the young.

That ought to make even Sierra Club members happy!

For our twenty-first-century sensibilities, the Old Testament law appears to contain an unwavering sense of justice that is carried out without pity or mercy. Nothing could be further from the truth. These days we seem to seek psychological explanations for virtually every human behavior. This conditioning plays an integral role in making the Old Testament legal system sound harsh to us. However, in the Old Testament, criminals and wrongdoers were not excused from the consequences of their crimes. They deserved just punishment, but the punishment had to be fair and fitting. Israel was a lawful society. Therefore, there were strict and clear penalties for law-breaking. Moreover, strict punishment aptly applied gave the perpetrator ample opportunity both to repent of his crime and to contemplate his life in light of eternity.

Swift Punishment

The Old Testament prescribed the death penalty for convicted murderers and the manner in which they were to be put to death. As we investigate what the Old Testament taught about the swift exercise of punishment against convicted felons, we shall notice that even though the issue of whether to execute stands front and center, there are also a number of added benefits for the community at large. That is to say, the swift execution of murderers in the Old Testament also carried with it a number of important components. Some of these included community safety, combating evil, an expression of the horror of murder, and future deterrence, just to mention a few. These will become more evident.

In the case of those convicted of capital crimes in the Old Testament, if the defendant was found guilty, the punishment was swift, decisive, and often the whole community took part. The result of this divinely-ordained procedure is manifold. First, the death of the convicted murderer is just. The punishment has been meted out according to a divine standard of right and wrong. Furthermore, with the death of the convicted murderer, the community is now safe from the evil person. He will never murder again. But there are still other advantages to His solution. The community is not only safe from the predator, but is cognizant of the fact that God's displeasure has been turned away. If the community had, for whatever reason, chosen not to execute the convicted murderer, they would have endured God's displeasure with them for not following His directives. Finally, by virtue of public execution, others contemplating murder might be deterred. The Israelites were confident that their strict law code protected both the guilty and the innocent in their land. The Israelites learned from the Lord that the execution of a person convicted of a capital crime is a way to protect their community from evil and its proliferation.

Like today, murder then was also a horrendous crime. Unlike today, however, once a person was convicted of murder, it was unthinkable that the evildoer would be allowed to live.

Modern secular humanists (or progressives, as they prefer to call themselves) do not understand the link between punishment and justice. They seek, in vain, for a cure for the convicted murderer, turning a blind eye and a deaf ear to the recidivism statistics. C.S. Lewis was quite insightful when he explained that the "concept of desert [what is justly deserved] is the only connecting link between punishment and justice."[30] This is an answer to the question of whether the death penalty is an actual deterrent. Certainly it is to the one executed. And the immeasurable part of the equation is – how many do observe that the state takes murder seriously and punishes it summarily and decide against the risk of getting executed themselves?

While some today are insistent that the execution of murderers is not a measurable deterrent, consider this: Dr. Isaac Ehrlich, an economic theorist from the University of Chicago, was given the opportunity to present his views on the effects of the death penalty to the U.S. Supreme Court.

> He compiled some impressive data, analyzing it according to modern methods of statistics, and concluded that, from 1933 to 1969, every execution of a murderer may have saved as many as seven or eight lives.

The theory behind his conclusions is

> that all human action is based on some assessment of costs and benefits. A predictable use of capital punishment is – or was – a cost of homicide, and when criminals were aware of this, there was a restraining effect upon the number of homicides committed.[31]

The Jewish radio talk show host, Dennis Prager, suggests that

> It is cosmic injustice to allow a murderer to keep his life. [He adds,] Killing murderers is society's only way to teach how horrible murder is. The only real way a society can express its revulsion at any criminal behavior is through the punishment it metes out. If murderers all got 10 years in prison and thieves all got 20 years in

prison, that would be society's way of saying that thievery is worse than murder. A society that kills murderers is saying that murder is more heinous a crime than a society that keeps all its murderers alive.[32]

When members of a community give sympathy to evil, evildoers gain power in that community and the community is negatively impacted. I cited the text from Ecclesiastes 8:11 previously, but in this setting it bears repeating:

Because the sentence against an evil deed is not executed speedily, the heart of the children of man is fully set to do evil.

All of us need to ponder this truth.

5

FROM THE

NEW TESTAMENT

SOCIETY in Biblical times and society in modern-day America seem to be ages and worlds apart. In a real sense, they are. Since we cannot understand a great deal of the New Testament apart from the Old, let me take a moment and briefly explain the relationship between the Old and New Testaments as well as where we are in American culture today.

Israel was a theocracy, a nation governed by laws given by God Himself. As such, in Old Testament times, church and state were, in a real sense, one. By this I do not mean that there was a one-to-one correspondence between church and state in the Old Testament. There was, however, very close proximity in the sense that the "rulers" were either appointed by God or by the people from within the covenant of grace. That is not the case in America today, although a case can be made that early in our history our jurisprudence was derived from Scripture. For example, initially our jurisprudence was founded on Common Law, which was more of a Bible-based system derived from England. The United States, however, is a representative republic governed by civil magistrates. Some of our federal, state, and local representatives claim to be believers, while others are avowed secularists/atheists. Currently in this country, there is a clearly traceable paradigm shift. At the outset, the Ten Commandments played a key role in shaping our laws. Gradually, there was a movement away from the Ten Commandments to what is called Natural Law. Today, with our relativism and repulsion among postmodernists against foundationalism,* we are left with only personal preference. This approach gives us no fixed compass for either individual or societal life. Americans have rejected God's transcendent law and supplanted it with man's variable statutory rule.

However, in New Testament times as well as in our time, there is still a need for the civil government to oversee the punishment of evil in our midst. Above, I have briefly outlined how modern society operates. Here we want to ask the question: What does God tell us in the New Testament about the requirements the Lord has laid on the elected and appointed governmental public officials? We shall now turn to the New Testament for insights Paul gives us in Romans 13, for it is precisely there that we hear of God's will for the New Testament Church as well as the onus that He places on Christian and non-Christian magistrates to carry out His will.

Romans 13:1-7

In Romans 13:4, the Apostle Paul defines the civil magistrate (ruling governor or prince) this way:

> He is God's servant for your good. But if you do wrong be afraid, for he does not bear the sword in vain...he is the servant of God, an avenger who carries out God's wrath on the wrongdoer.

Clearly, this text indicates that the government bears "the sword"

---

* epistemological theory, that some beliefs are justified by reference to others more basic.

and is responsible to execute justice in the land. In the New Testament, the word "sword" is frequently associated with death and was the instrument of execution.* This begs the question: "What are the implications God's justice has for the modern state?" to which Vern Poythress, a Calvinist New Testament theologian, responds from a Christian perspective, "God has always been Lord and Ruler of the world and everything in it,"[1] since the beginning of time.

When the New Testament describes state authorities, the presupposition is that, just as in the Old Testament, these rulers derive their authority from God. The text under scrutiny is a classic case in point. Verse 4 points to the legitimate function of the state authorities to punish the wrongdoer. The Old Testament also requires both Israelite kings and judges to rule according to God's standards of justice (Deut. 25:2; 2 Chron. 9:8; Isa. 10:1; Jer. 22:2-3; 1 Kings 2:3) and others (Prov. 16:12; 29:4; 31:4-5; Ps. 82).

> Since all authority derives from Christ, all authorities are answerable to Him. All actions of the state ought to conform to God's standards of justice revealed in Christ.[2]

Nevertheless, there are differences. Even though the state, modern or otherwise, derives its authority from God, it cannot and must not act in the same way as the church. This is an essential difference to grasp. The task of the state is not to show mercy, but rather to execute justice. The state is, therefore,

> firmly confined to earth. Even though it has divine authority, it does not give us access to heaven.[3]

When the Apostle Paul explains the state's role in the execution of justice, Poythress states that he is, at the same time, reminding us of the following:

---

* cf. Matt. 26:52; Luke 21:24; Acts 12:2; 16:27; Heb. 11:34, 37; Rev. 13:10.

> For the criminal's own good the criminal must feel the
> weight of God's preliminary punishment. He must be
> reminded of the more ultimate consequences of crime
> when God's last judgment comes.[4]

These truths are quite often overlooked. The helpful reminder,
however, is first that the criminal must receive a foretaste of a
much more serious punishment and second, he must be pointed to the more ultimate, eternal consequences of lawlessness.
Punishments meted out by the state help make these points.
Poythress puts it this way:

> Thus we may say that state-supervised punishments
> present a kind of shadow of God's judgment, while Chris-
> tians through the gospel present the reality to which
> that shadow points. That is, Christians present the real-
> ity of Christ's penal death and the reality of hell awaiting
> those who do not put their trust in Christ. *When human
> beings have injured other human beings, both the shadow
> and the reality need to be presented.*[5]

Those who desire to do away with the death penalty are, either
consciously or unconsciously, dispensing with the much-needed
reminder in our society of the consequences of sin. God enjoins
capital punishment for convicted murderers, and we must not
shrink from applying what God has commanded.

In summary then, Poythress gives us three useful guidelines
for just state punishments:

> [First,] the state derives its authority from God, is an-
> swerable to God for its actions, and must endeavor to
> embody in its laws and its punishments the standards
> of God's justice.
>
> [Second,] the state has a limited authority, an authority
> over a limited territory on earth.

This is an essential and necessary point, especially in light of the fact that there have been some Christians in the past who have argued for, say, the non-execution of convicted criminals when they made a profession of Christ as Savior. The state

> cannot release criminals or pardon them on the basis of Christ's sacrifice, because access to Christ is by way of faith in Christ and spiritual union with Him.
>
> [Third and finally,] the state deals with injuries against other human beings, not injuries against God.
>
> [Therefore, in the fulfilling of its duties,] the state must not insist on attaining divine perfection.[6]

Perfection was not attainable in Old Testament and New Testament times, nor is it today. What is required of the state is to insure that due legal process is used in rendering justice and that no penalty ought to be executed until guilt has been established. In other words, the accused is innocent until proven guilty.

This text of Holy Scripture, in Romans 13:1-7, has been given to us by God and is applicable for us today. There are modern scholars who would disagree with that statement and who believe that this text has nothing to do with Christians. The influence of these liberal scholars has crept into certain sectors of modern Christianity. While scholarship can be a valuable resource, good scholarship bows before Scripture. Scripture does not bow before scholarship. Therefore, when we study the Bible, we need to let the words of Scripture speak with authority. Each text must speak for itself. If we need more clarity, we can compare the text in question with other pertinent portions of the Word of God. That is the correct way to look at Romans 13:1-7.

First, then, we need to understand the context in which Romans 13 is written. In chapter 12 of Romans, the Apostle Paul urged believers to "present their bodies as a living sacrifice, holy and acceptable to God" (Rom. 12:1). He also told them to "be transformed by the renewal" of their minds (v. 12:2). At the end of the chapter, he discusses the attitudes they needed to build in their relationships with others, even those who persecuted them. He finishes the chapter with this command: "Do not be overcome by evil, but overcome evil with good" (v. 12:21). It is following this powerful statement that Paul wrote about the relationship Christians have with the civil government.

When Paul wrote his letter to the Romans, the church at Rome, which had many Jewish congregants, was under the civil rule of the Roman government. That could not have been easy and there were many struggles attached to this situation for these believers. Paul is reminding both the civil government and Christians of their mutual, reciprocal duties.

At the outset, Paul explains the place of the civil government after he tells the church that "there is no authority except from God, and those that exist have been instituted by God" (Rom. 13:1). William Hendriksen, late reformed scholar, author, and preacher, provided an excellent perspective when he wrote,

> All civil magistrates, in the final analysis, owe their ap-
> pointments and right to govern to God. It is by His will
> and in His providence that they have been appointed
> to maintain order, encourage well-doing, and punish
> wrong-doing.[7]

Like it or not, rulers and government leaders are appointed by God and must answer to God – eventually – for how they govern.

In the next verse, Paul addresses the believers in Rome in this fashion:

> Therefore whoever resists the authorities resists what
> God has appointed, and those who resist will incur
> judgment (13:2).

For Christians living under a godless and powerful government like first century Rome that is a difficult concept to accept. Does that mean that we are to *always* obey the government laws and wishes? Since "always" is a small word with a large reach, the obvious answer is "no." When the government requires that we violate part of the revealed will of God to obey a law of the state, then we are duty bound to disobey (cf. Dan. 3:18; Acts 5:29). Paul certainly understood in his time how tyrannical and dictatorial certain governing officials could be.

Actually, this text speaks more to governing authorities than to individuals for Paul is saying "that all human authority is derived from God's authority...."[8] He is not referring to particular heads of state (Nero, Domitian, etc.) but rather calling the state to acknowledge that its authority is derived from God (cf. John 19:11).

I live in the beautiful state of California. My state is currently governed by one of the most liberal, if not *the* most liberal, state legislatures in the country. The politically-correct socialistic political atmosphere in our state tremendously influences the lives of California citizens. Our taxes are high and our properties are over-valued. Our state-managed health care and social systems are in shambles. Our jails are filled to overflowing. Nevertheless, the citizens of California, including the Christians, are still responsible for following the mandates found in Romans 13.

Politicians of all stripes, dictators, and heads of state have far too often either forgotten or ignored that they have been appointed to be *servants* (v. 4). When leaders and governing magistrates fail to understand that their authority is given to them by God and not derived from their own persons, they lack the perspective to exercise properly the authority that has been divinely given to them. The perfection of the state is God's business; the responsibility and proper fulfillment of the office of civil magistrate is the task of man. As Christians, we are called upon to obey our civil government unless it requires us to violate God's words.

Not every government will serve the purposes of the Gospel; in fact, few will. There will be varying levels of fulfilling the God-given mandate. Some countries and individual states will be more or less faithful, others will be bad, others worse, and still some others will be *very* evil. However, we see in Paul's life that even though he was personally mistreated by less than ideal governments, he was consistently willing to put himself in danger for the sake of the Gospel (cf. Acts 16:19-24; 2 Cor. 11:25). Paul knew that because God graciously governs all of His creation and because civil servants lead by His appointment, God has the power to use all leaders, even unbelieving ones, to accomplish all that He has purposed. It is not government that ultimately protects and provides for people; it is God who does that. No one falls outside of His rule, not even unbelieving government officials. We certainly learn much from Paul's example.

At the end of Romans 12, Paul discusses the basic theme of good and evil (vv. 9, 17, and 21). In chapter 13, it seems that Paul is now depicting the role of government with that same theme in mind. In Romans 13:3 he writes: "For rulers are not a terror to good conduct, but to bad." In verses 4-6, he speaks of the magistrate not bearing "the sword in vain" and being "an avenger who carries out God's wrath." Paul clearly describes both restraint and punishment of evil as the primary role of the magistrate. The word Paul uses here for "sword" (*máchaira*) was employed earlier in the letter in 8:35 to indicate death.

About the relationship between Romans 13:4 and the continuation of the death penalty, Vern Poythress writes,

> In particular, the mention of the sword in Romans 13:4 indicates the legitimacy of the continuation of the death penalty." [Moreover,] The death penalty is therefore still the appropriate penalty for murder. [Therefore,] Principles of general equity, as well as the specific content of Genesis 9:6, clearly enjoin the death penalty as a universal penalty for murder, even if the murder is unconnected with the promised holy land.[9]

It seems that Paul is indicating that the job of government is to punish wrongdoing and disobedience, even if the act of disobedience means a punishment of death.

Paul also speaks of those who "do wrong" (*kakòn*) (v. 4). Very simply put, we are to obey God first and foremost, but also obey the civil magistrate except where man's laws require us to violate God's. We are to obey the speed limit even if we think it is too slow, to stop at stop signs even though we are in a hurry, to control ourselves and not steal even though we would like to have what our neighbor has, to care for our neighbor's well-being even though we don't particularly want to, to refrain from murdering someone even though it is hard to contain our hatred for them, and the like. And if we break the law, we deserve the just consequences of the law according to our wrongdoing.

With such a grave responsibility, the state must make every effort to differentiate rightly between good and evil. Those who are responsible to judge must recognize evil for what it is. God Himself, who gives every judge his or her power, holds that judge accountable. He or she must rightly and precisely interpret the law of the land. In spite of the judge's personal or political preferences, justice must prevail. The Source of all justice requires it. There is an interesting concept given in v. 4 that needs further exposition and explanation.

The State Must Possess an Awareness of Right and Wrong, Good and Evil.

The government is called "the servant of God" in our text. To be a *just* servant of God, the civil magistrate must possess a heightened awareness of what is right and wrong; what is good and evil. Society today has a degree of moral awareness, but the ability of people in and outside of government to distinguish right and wrong has been buried under an avalanche of politically-correct, liberal, feel-good claptrap. The fogginess about right and wrong, good and evil has taken its toll on capital punishment.

Nevertheless, it is Paul's assumption that the state must have some moral consciousness regarding good and evil and to be able to judge correctly between the two. This also is part of the state's God-ordained mandate. In verse 4, Paul's argument is based upon the fact that the state knows what is "wrong" and "right" behavior. The magistrate carries out God's wrath on the *wrongdoer*. It is a legitimate argument that even the nonbeliever knows this difference because God has implanted it in his heart (cf. Rom. 2:14-15).*

With this as background, we want to take a look in the next chapters at some of the objections raised by secularists and some Christians against the death penalty.

A Summary from the Westminster Confession of Faith

The Westminster Confession of Faith emphasizes the truth we have been referring to in regard to the place of the civil magistrate and the responsibilities that he bears in capital punishment. It addresses the issue in chapter twenty-three (*Of the Civil Magistrate*), section one, when it states the following:

---

* For when the Gentiles, who do not have the law, by nature do what the law requires, they are a law to themselves, even though they do not have the law. They show that the work of the law is written on their hearts.

> God, the supreme Lord and King of all the world, has ordained civil magistrates to be, under Him, over the people, for His own glory, and the public good: and, to this end, has armed them with the power of the sword, for the defense and encouragement of them that are good, and for the punishment of evil doers.

Section three draws a clear line between the civil magistrates and the church.

> Civil magistrates may not assume to themselves the administration of the Word and sacraments; or the power of the keys of the kingdom of heaven; or, *in the least*, interfere in matters of faith. (*Emphasis added.*)

The Confession provides us with a clear and comprehensive summary of what God expects from our elected and appointed officials as well as the distinction between the duties of the church and the state.

6

ADDRESSING THE
SECULAR OBJECTIONS TO
CAPITAL PUNISHMENT

Most objections to capital punishment by the opponents are based on views pertaining to the Eighth Amendment to the Constitution, which protects the individual from cruel and unusual punishment. This amendment also guarantees protection from forms of punishment that are not in proportion to the crime committed.[1]

Secularists (and some Christians) have developed a kind of "humanitarian" concern about the wanton and inordinate infliction of pain and suffering involved with the death penalty, therefore, they oppose capital punishment, maintaining it is also out of proportion to the crime. The reasons offered for such choices vary from excessive pain inflicted on the one to be executed to a visceral aversion to capital punishment. In my home state of California, some have objected to the pain inflicted by lethal injection, totally disregarding the pain that the convicted murderer inflicted on his victim. Others simply declare the death penalty to be inhumane, as we shall see below. The simple declaration is made that capital punishment is a relic from the early, rudimentary days of penology, and that any state-authorized killing is immoral. These are standard responses in many of the liberal state institutions where Americans send their children to become educated.

In passing, it is interesting to note that when the Bill of Rights was written in 1789, which included the Eighth Amendment, *every* state allowed the death penalty. As of this writing, however, thirty-eight states as well as the federal government have statutes authorizing the death penalty by one of five methods: lethal injection, electrocution, lethal gas, hanging, and firing squad. Many of those states have laws allowing for multiple or alternative methods of execution, depending upon the convict's choice, the date of execution or sentence, or the possibility that the method might be found unconstitutional. Eighteen states authorize lethal injection as the sole method of execution. Eighteen others provide for lethal injection as the primary or alternative method of execution. Only two states – Alabama and Nebraska – currently use electrocution as the sole method of execution. No states provide for lethal gas, hanging, or a firing squad as the *sole* method of execution. Current death penalty procedure requires that the execution take place inside the walls of a state prison before sunrise.

The purpose of this paragraph is to give you, the reader, a grasp on how the state views capital punishment and allow you to compare it with what Scripture teaches. Twelve states have no death penalty at all. When we compare this with the Biblical mandates, it there any wonder that our land is "polluted"? Even among the states that have laws on the books regarding capital punishment, few of them execute convicted criminals in a timely fashion. In some states, such as California, the law is on the books, but the greatest cause of death for those on death row is old age; a distant second is suicide, and a very distant third is actual penal execution.

All of the following objections argue against the state's exercising its authority to mete out justice to condemned murderers. But are these objections correct? We will determine the answer to that question by applying the Biblical principles we have just learned.

Initially, however, I have a general comment to make. Earlier, we looked at the Scriptural distinction John Calvin made between killing and murder. He reminded us that *all murder is killing, but not all killing is murder.* When the death penalty issue is raised, there are inevitably people who insist that capital punishment is wrong because the Bible forbids killing. That is a fallacious argument. Therefore, before we begin to examine the objections, note this by way of summary: Murder is an illegal act; a horrendous crime. We must remember that when the civil magistrate executes a convicted murderer, that is not the crime of *murder.* Execution is an act of *justice* permitted by God and the laws of the state. The magistrate simply has the God-ordained responsibility to carry out the law. Magistrates, like soldiers and policemen, are not guilty of murder in the normal functions of their duties requiring lethal force.

The following, then, are some of the most common arguments secularists (and some Christians) use to oppose the death penalty. In order to be fair, I will not construct a "straw man" based on conjuring up what the secularists might say. Rather, I will use the words of a secular opponent to the death penalty, Dr. Hugo Adam Bedau.* For fairness, I will state the case of the secularists using their words. After I have allowed the "abolitionists" to expound their case, I will then respond to their assertions. I will discuss their objections under eight separate headings.

---

* In addition to the online article available from Dr. Bedau (Fletcher Professor of Philosophy, Tufts University, Medford, MA), he has also written a book entitled *The Death Penalty in America* (NY: Oxford University Press, 1992). In these writings, he can be seen to be an ardent "abolitionist" as far as capital punishment is concerned.

Objection #1:

The death penalty violates the constitutional ban against cruel and unusual punishment, the guarantee of due process of law, and equal protection under the law.

Opponents to the death penalty – Christians and non-Christians alike – believe that it is "a barbaric practice, out of place in the modern world and unconstitutional as cruel and inhuman punishment." Scott B. Rae, PH.D., a Christian ethics professor at Biola University, also notes that some uninformed Christians believe that the death penalty violates "the ethics of Jesus." These Christians are convinced that the cry for justice is "only a façade for revenge,"[2] which makes capital punishment inconsistent with Jesus' teachings. We shall examine these objections as we proceed. Taking a realistic look at the organization known as the American Civil Liberties Union is an apt place to begin.

The American Civil Liberties Union

The American Civil Liberties Union (ACLU), a bulwark of secularism, holds that the imposition of the death penalty is inconsistent with the fundamental values of democracy.* In the judgment of the ACLU, the state should not claim for itself the right to kill human beings, especially when it kills with premeditation and ceremony, under color of law and in our names. When society exercises the death penalty, it does so, according to the ACLU, in an arbitrary and *discriminatory* fashion. Capital punishment is, therefore, an intolerable denial of civil liberties. In other words, the ACLU believes that there are hardly any circumstances – if any – that justify capital punishment.

---

* Former National Organization for Women (NOW) Los Angeles chapter leader Tammy Bruce, a lesbian Democrat, writes the following concerning this organization: "One of the most damaging Leftist entities in this nation right now is the so-called American Civil Liberties Union (ACLU). This is the group recognized by thoughtful Americans everywhere as Base Camp for the Left's nihilistic agenda." (*The New American Revolution*, [NY: HarperCollins, 2005], 210.)

Rae informs us that the ACLU's mantra is,

> No crime, however heinous, and no view of criminal punishment can be adequate grounds for sentencing anyone to death.[3]

And Bedau further maintains that, citizens are to continue to seek to prevent executions and to abolish capital punishment by litigation, legislation, commutation, or by the weight of a renewed public outcry against this *brutal and brutalizing institution*.[4] Rae says, nevertheless,

> The latest polls in America indicate that the majority favors the death penalty in principle; that is, most Americans oppose abolishing all capital punishment as many European nations have done.[5]

Robert Bork (legal scholar, author, former U.S. Circuit Judge; nominated to the Supreme Court by President Ronald Reagan but not confirmed), is more trenchant in his ACLU-criticism. He writes,

> There exists in this culture a significant disjunction in attitudes. The same people and organizations manage simultaneously to adopt positions of extreme moralism and extreme moral relativism. If one had to choose one organization to illustrate this feature of modern left-liberal culture, it would be the American Civil Liberties Union. Its positions resemble those of many other public interest groups, and it is the primary litigating arm of the adversary of culture.[6]

Bork cites William Donohue's book *The Politics of the American Civil Liberties Union* (1985), which is a seminal work on the liberalism of the ACLU.[7] Therefore, when it comes to the death penalty, America is locked in a titanic struggle.

The burden of proof here is upon those in opposition to

delineate precisely how capital punishment actually violates the constitutional ban on cruel and unusual punishment. Apparently thirty-eight states as well as federal regulations do not agree with the ACLU. What are, then, the most common arguments put forward by the ACLU and other proponents for the abolition of the death penalty? For the remainder of this book, our focus will be on examining and rebutting those arguments.

The Death Penalty as Cruel and Unusual Punishment

Hugo Bedau, one of the modern proponents of the abolition of the death penalty, calls capital punishment

> a relic of the earliest days of penology, when slavery, branding, and other corporal punishments were commonplace. Like those other barbaric practices, executions have no place in a civilized society.[8]

Of course, a mere referral to history doesn't make the case. There is, however, substantial historical precedence for capital punishment in America. Therefore, something more is needed. This "more" is ostensibly accomplished in another fashion. How is that accomplished? To trigger compassion further, opponents of the death penalty sometimes describe the *manner* in which a person dies when he or she is executed. Such descriptions cause the hearer to forget that the individual being executed is a convicted murderer who has caused someone else to meet a terrifying death. Death, it is argued, is an enemy to life no matter how it comes, whether by murder, by execution, or by natural causes. It is ugly and comes upon its victim strangely and with difficulty, even in its most gentle state.

But there is still more to be said than the secularists are willing to say. Their appeal to the Eighth Amendment overlooks (intentionally?) the Fifth Amendment, which makes a case *for* the death penalty. It reads,

> No person shall be held to answer for a capital, or
> otherwise infamous crime, unless on a presentment or
> indictment of a Grand Jury....

The clear assumption is that there are capital crimes which
need to be adjudicated. The Fifth Amendment continues and
requires "due process of law" for all. Therefore, it is, at best,
very inconsistent on the secularists' part to ignore the obvious
implications of the Fifth Amendment in their arguments.

We live in a day and age when we have all but forgotten that
the United States has a constitution. In the 2008 presidential
campaign, there was scant mention of this document by any of
the candidates, with notable exception. Forgetting our founding
documents, we have simultaneously forgotten that, as Kevin
Ring, former counsel to the Senate Constitution Subcommittee
and editor of *Scalia Dissents,* reports,

> The Constitution of the United States expressly refers
> to the death penalty.

What is more,

> Among historians, there is no serious doubt as to whether
> the death penalty was an accepted form of punishment
> when the Constitution was adopted.[9]

When our Bill of Rights was written (1789), every state allowed
capital punishment. How was the Eighth Amendment understood from a historical perspective? David Forte, Professor
of Law, Cleveland-Marshall College of Law, Cleveland, Ohio,
describes the history of the amendment this way:

> Although the issue is disputed, the weight of scholarly
> opinion indicates that the ban on cruel and unusual
> punishment in the 1689 English Bill of Rights applied
> only to punishments not authorized by Parliament.

This points us to the truth that capital punishment was an accepted means of punishment for certain heinous, egregious crimes. Forte says, the reservations on cruel and unusual punishments by the colonists

> was that the ban applied to torturous punishments, such as pillorying, disemboweling, decapitation, and drawing and quartering.[10]

But any reasonable reading of the Eighth Amendment draws our attention to three clear and distinct aspects. As Rae states,

> [First, it] protects individuals from cruel and unusual punishment. Specifically, it provides protection from the wanton and unnecessary infliction of pain.
>
> [Second,] the Eighth Amendment protects a person from punishment that is out of proportion to the crime committed.
>
> [Finally,] the Constitution protects individuals from punishment without due process of law.[11]

This comports with common sense, but there were storms brewing on the horizon. It should be duly noted that all three of these criteria are met when the death penalty is administered in the United States.

About halfway through the twentieth century, some new winds were blowing in the United States and they would be harbingers of a wave of liberalism that would sweep across the country. Kevin Gutzman, American historian, writes,

> The Supreme Court of the 1950s and 1960s often gave the impression that it had found a new Constitution only marginally related to the old one. The Warren Court of 1954–1969 was the great age of judicial legislation, when American constitutional law was remade in the image of the liberal intellectual.

And this being the case, it is not too difficult to understand that the liberal-intellectual resistance to capital punishment is not something that sprang up overnight, but rather has a history going back almost six decades. Indeed,

> The federal courts have been in the business for many decades now of remaking the American law of criminal punishment.[12]

The first challenge to the constitutionality of the death penalty did not occur until 1972. I want to take a moment and outline what happened in 1972 and in the years that followed because it is germane to our topic. The Supreme Court of the United States ruled twice on the issue of capital punishment in the 1970s (1972 and 1976). On June 29, 1972, in *Furman v. Georgia*, it was ruled – by a split decision – that the imposition of the death penalty in the states of Texas and Georgia constituted violations of both the Eighth and Fourteenth Amendments to the U.S. Constitution.* When this decision was handed down, Scalia commented,

> the Supreme Court effectively suspended use of capital punishment on the grounds that its arbitrary administration violated the Eighth Amendment's prohibition of "cruel and unusual punishments."[13]

It can be correctly stated that in 1972, a "paradigm shift" moved enough justices away from being strict originalists (those who interpret the Constitution according to the original intent of the framers of it), who interpreted law, to those who ruled from the bench according to their own worldviews and presuppositions. This teaches us the following lesson: A "liberal" judge will almost inevitably render a liberal opinion. The same

---

* The Eighth Amendment forbids cruel and unusual punishments. The Fourteenth Amendment requires equal protection under the law.

is true of conservative justices rendering conservative opinions. This is America and this is how our country operates. My point in all this is that virtually everyone has some kind of bias and predilection and it will appear in the different opinions of even Supreme Court justices. Therefore, we should keep in mind that our discussions surrounding the death penalty and other ethical issues are not merely skirmishes in the "culture war," but also ideological struggles, where the opposition has a "dog in the fight" and also has a "stomach for the fight."

In 1992, Justice Sandra Day O'Connor, who had imbibed deeply from the Warren Court legacy and understanding of the Constitution, wrote that the Court needed to apply not the law, but the "evolving standards of decency that mark the progress of a maturing society." (*Hudson v. McMillian* [1992]).* Justice O'Connor's statement was at once both telling and arrogant. She was indicating that the *Court's* "standards of decency" was the final word. Moreover, this type of thinking opened the door for left-of-center politicians to begin "ruling from the bench" by securing the appointments of justices that were not strict originalists and who infused their rulings with their own life and worldview. This, of course, is quite wrong. Robert Bork reminds us that

> There is no faintest hint in the Constitution...that the judiciary shares any of the legislative or executive power.[14]

Early nineteenth century Associate Justice of the Supreme Court and a professor of law at Harvard, Joseph Story, wrote in his commentaries on the Constitution that

> A constitution of government is addressed to the common sense of the people; and never was designed for trials of logical skill or visionary speculation.[15]

---

* The words, "evolving standards of decency that mark the progress of a maturing society," were drawn verbatim from Chief Justice Earl Warren's words in *Trop v. Dulles* (1954).

6 Addressing the Secular Objections

The modern Court has disregarded Story's admonition.

Fast forward to 1994. Justices Harry Blackmun, William Brennan, and Thurgood Marshall dissented from the Court's decision not to consider an appeal brought by a convicted murderer. It was their settled conviction that "capital punishment always violated the Eighth Amendment ban on cruel and unusual punishments."[16] These men based their decision on their interpretation of "evolving standards of decency" of which they were both judge and jury. In short, their thinking and actions promoted the idea that they were more intelligent and knew better than other courts as well as the American people, and for that matter, the Law-Giver our Creator. Apparently, they had "evolved" more than Americans at large.

> [Justice Blackmun] used his dissent in this case to announce his conclusion that the death penalty, because of its imperfect application, was *always* "cruel and unusual" and, thus, unconstitutional.*

Employing emotional language, Blackmun waxed eloquent regarding how the defendant, Bruce Callins, would be put to death. Kevin Ring, records Blackmun's words:

> Intravenous tubes attached to his arms will carry the instrument of death, a toxic fluid designed specifically for the purpose of killing human beings. The witnesses, standing a few feet away, will behold Callins, no longer a defendant, an appellant, or a petitioner, but a man strapped to a gurney, and seconds away from extinction.

This is precisely the kind of words that is specifically designed to induce emotional reaction rather than reasonable response. Ring continues,

---

* According to Kevin Ring, (ed.) in *Scalia Dissents*, 144. And Ring adds, that Blackmun, "In a memorable phrase, he said he would no longer 'tinker with the machinery of death,'"145.

Whatever Blackmun's motivation, Justice Scalia noted that the lethal injection of Callins – a "convicted murderer" – seemed "enviable" compared with the brutal deaths suffered by Callins's and other killers' victims.[17]

In writing his concurring opinion to *Callins v. Collins* (1994), Justice Scalia rebutted Blackmun at length. Scalia insisted that the Fifth Amendment was still in full force in the United States and then included the Eighth Amendment in his concurring opinion when he stated,

> This clearly permits the death penalty to be imposed, and establishes beyond doubt that the death penalty is not one of the "cruel and unusual punishments" prohibited by the Eighth Amendment.[18]

What does the Eighth Amendment say? It is rather short and is easy to understand. It reads,

> Excessive bail shall not be required, nor excessive fines imposed, nor cruel and unusual punishments inflicted.

Historically, according to *The Heritage Guide to the Constitution*,

> The text of the Eighth Amendment derives from the 1689 English Bill of Rights, redacted in the Virginia Declaration of Rights and recommended by the Virginia ratifying convention.[19]

Modern pundits, however, have forced the Eighth Amendment to say something that it does not say, namely that the death penalty constitutes the infliction of cruel and unusual punishment.

For the convicted murderer, execution is merely the just penalty for his crime. Yes, there is probably some pain involved, but with the modern procedures, that pain is minimal. Capital punishment is, after all, *death* as well as the *punishment* for the willful, malicious, and premeditated taking of another's life. Some among the elitist intellectuals believe that convicted murderers, who committed heinous crimes, should face neither reprisal nor retribution by the state. Few, it seems, want to face the stark and gruesome reality of the deaths of murder *victims*. Justice Scalia, in his concurring opinion against Justice Blackmun cited the "case of the eleven-year-old girl raped by four men and then killed by stuffing her panties down her throat."[20]

Being joined by Justice Clarence Thomas in a dissenting opinion (*Atkins v. Virginia* [2002]), the two men complain that the death of Airman Eric Nesbitt at the hands of Daryl Renard Atkins should have carried the death penalty with it. Why? The facts of the case are that Atkins and a cohort, after spending the day drinking alcohol and smoking marijuana, drove to a convenience store intending to rob a customer at gunpoint. Nesbitt was the customer, who was in the proverbial wrong place at the wrong time. Atkins and his accomplice abducted Nesbitt and drove to a nearby ATM, where they forced him to withdraw $200. They then drove Nesbitt to a deserted area, where, according to testimony from the cohort, the man begged for his life. Scalia and Thomas point out that "Atkins ordered Nesbitt out of the vehicle and, after he had taken only a few steps, shot him one, two, three, four, five, six, seven, eight times in the thorax, chest, abdomen, arms, and legs." In this particular case, the jury also heard testimony about Mr. Atkins's sixteen prior felony convictions for robbery, attempted robbery, abduction, use of a firearm, and maiming. In other words, Atkins was a violent man with a number of prior felony arrests. In addition, the jury heard of how Atkins had "slapped a gun across another victim's face, clubbed her in the head with it, knocked her to the ground, and then helped her up, only to shoot her in the stomach."[21] In light of these facts, sentencing Atkins to death hardly constitutes cruel and unusual punishment, but justice.

It seems, therefore, that for our modern culture, when it comes to the death penalty, there is a twofold desire: First, many secularists believe that in spite of the pain and suffering inflicted by the murderer upon his or her victim(s), *painless* death is the imperative criterion for meting out retributive justice. Therefore, the first objective of opponents to the death penalty is virtually to eliminate all pain from the method of execution. Nevertheless, it should also be agreed that we will never be able to eliminate all pain because of the nature of dying.

Second, people like Professor Bedau, the Warren Court, and others believe that all methods of execution, even lethal injection, are "an expression of the *absolute* power of the state over the helpless individual."[22] We should keep in mind, however, that the state does not possess absolute power. It does, however, possess *derived* power, from God and from the people. Abolitionists feel that the convicted and condemned murderer is the "helpless individual" or "victim." He or she is "helpless" because he must submit to the desires of society that laws are enforced, especially laws concerning the taking of another person's life. Exercising its derived authority, the state "purges evil from its midst." Whereas the first desire of opponents to capital punishment is to eliminate pain, their second and presumed true objective is to eliminate the death penalty altogether.

Before we move on, I want to draw our attention to a glaring inconsistency among those who believe capital punishment constitutes cruel and unusual punishment. Many of the opponents of the death penalty also favor active *euthanasia* (mercy killing). If lethal injection can be essentially painless – and it can be – isn't this the same procedure recommended by those seeking euthanasia rights in this country? The advocates of active euthanasia view that "procedure" as an act of mercy, but the virtually identical procedure, when applied to the death penalty is no longer mercy, but rather cruel and unusual punishment. There is a crass, ideological double standard applied where what is favored by progressive secularist humanists recommends a person being painlessly put out of misery, while the death penalty by lethal injection violates the Eighth Amendment.[23]

Even though opponents of capital punishment object to the execution of convicted murderers, they are quick to say that they favor no one in particular and have no misplaced sympathy for criminals in general. They simply believe in equal treatment under the law for everyone. They claim not to want to upset the families and loved ones of murder victims. Generously, Professor Bedau concedes that most of the family members who lost a loved one to the murderer want to exact some kind of satisfaction or retribution and may favor the death penalty. The objection to Bedau's explanation is partially true. For example, if a loved one has been murdered, those left behind to experience the pain of loss plus the anguish of knowing that the loved one was brutally murdered understandably want the state to take retribution on the convicted murderer.

Bedau further explains, however, that it is not that opponents to capital punishment think that murder is somehow okay. Rather, they simply believe there are better, more justified remedies than the death penalty such as life imprisonment without the possibility of parole. This last approach presents a rather heavy burden on the taxpayer. Statistics differ somewhat, but it is generally conceded that it costs approximately $30,000 per year to meet the needs of one prisoner on death row.

> Assuming an average of thirty years spent in prison, taxpayers will spend about $900,000 per inmate who is serving a life sentence.[24]

Of course, Professor Bedau does not substantiate his assertions precisely because he cannot. Ultimately, however, what we're left with in his ethics is a man-made solution that is in direct opposition to a God-ordained prescription. In addition, Bedau's position makes no mention of the violence and ghastly details that accompany murder, as we observed in the prior examples. While the secularists may disagree with capital punishment, from a Christian perspective the death penalty is a well-conceived and solidly Biblical Christian position. Moreover, by this time it should be clear that both historically and in terms of the modern methods of execution, capital punishment does not constitute cruel and unusual punishment as Bedau seems to intimate.

In addition, one must wonder how capital punishment can be a violation of equal protection under the law if it is only applied to *convicted murders,* all of whom have actually broken the law. The Fifth Amendment to the U.S. Constitution reminds us that,

> No person shall be held to answer for a *capital,* or otherwise infamous crime, unless on a presentment or indictment of a Grand Jury....

All on death row have had a trial by jury and have been found guilty. This first objection from Professor Bedau is specious and misleading.

We have taken some time to elaborate on the first objection to capital punishment, since it was necessary to lay a groundwork that will serve us well throughout the remainder of our commentary dealing with the most common objections to the death penalty.

Objection #2:
Capital punishment is arbitrary and irrevocable.

Opponents of the death penalty sometimes argue that capital punishment denies due process of law because it is *arbitrary* and *irrevocable.*[25] By "arbitrary," they do not mean that a person is randomly chosen to be executed. They are simply referring to what they perceive to be prejudice or racial profiling concerning wrong doers. To defend their opinion, they point to the fact that even though blacks represent only about 15–20% of the population of the United States, approximately 51% of death-row inmates are black. Secularists and some Christians contend that more blacks than whites are sentenced to die, not because more blacks commit capital crimes, but precisely because of the color of their skin. In other words, capital punishment is largely a racial prejudice according to its detractors. Among these critics are those who claim that America is a country where no one in a minority gets a fair and even break. In a separate article, Bedau cites Supreme Court Justice William O. Douglas who once quipped,

> One searches our chronicles in vain for the execution of any member of the affluent strata of this society.
>
> [He continues,] All the sociological evidence points to the conclusion that the death penalty is the poor man's justice; hence the slogan, "Those without the capital get the punishment."[26]

As far as the second objection is concerned, it is true that the death penalty is "irrevocable" since once it is carried out, it cannot be *undone*. Because of its finality, secularists and some Christians argue that it is possible that some innocent party could wrongfully be put to death and we wouldn't know it until it was too late, if we ever knew at all. They believe it would be far better to allow people to spend life in prison rather than to execute one innocent individual. But is this accusation true? A good case can be made that a lifetime of uselessness constitutes cruel and unusual punishment. This is an argument that cuts both ways. Moreover, life sentences without the possibility of parole can subject the perpetrator to incredible and unspeakable brutality and the "injustice" in the way inmates run their own subculture. The most substantial objection to this argument, however, is that it makes no provision for the Christian voice. Prisons in America are typically filled to overflowing, while, with the exception of the cities of refuge, a person will search the Old Testament in vain trying to locate a text that speaks of prison. In the New Testament, we understand that the prisons described there were the product of Roman law.

While it is true that there have been highly unusual instances where convicted but innocent parties sitting on death row have been proven to be not guilty, the "mistakes-will-be-made" argument oddly cuts both ways in a finite and fallible world. Sometimes murderers who were actually and clearly guilty escaped their just penalty because of loopholes and prosecutorial errors that allowed them to go free. Ernest van den Haag, Professor of Jurisprudence and Public Policy, Fordham University, New York, writing in the same book, takes the opposite side of the argument from Bedau but concedes that "over a long enough period, miscarriages of justice will occur even in capital cases."[27] This is part of the process, but it does not make the case that it is far better to allow thousands of convicted murderers to live simply because of the outside chance that one innocent person might be put to death. Innocents die daily in the United States. But accidental convictions of innocents have been greatly reduced by better science including incontrovertible DNA evidence. Just as there is an inconsistency among those who promote active euthanasia, but are opposed to capital punishment, there is also an inconsistency among those who fear an innocent might be wrongly executed, yet are unconcerned when millions of "innocents" are murdered every year by abortion on demand.

Yes, mistakes can be made – because we are human beings. Yet, should we use the *possibility of mistakes* by lawyers and judges as a reason to eliminate all trials? The short answer is "No." This is merely a secular attempt to eliminate the death penalty. Deuteronomy 17:8-13 provides us with an example of how difficult cases were decided according to God's law. According to Scripture, those in authority heard the case, consulted, and declared a verdict. No doubt, the whole of Old Testament Scripture was brought to bear in the decision-making process. The verdict, however, was incontrovertible and failure to comply with the verdict handed down was itself punishable by death (v. 12). There was no guarantee that fallible men, using God's infallible standard, would be one hundred percent correct one hundred percent of the time. This was, however, God's will and way for his people. Also, connected to this text are two other important, indispensable facets: First, there is the command to purge the evil from the midst of the people; and, second, the entire community would hear, fear, and not act presumptuously again (v. 3). If we returned to the Biblical model and, in murder cases, required two eyewitnesses who could testify as to what truly happened, we would create less room for error in our court rooms.

Part of the Biblical model is that in all things we ground our actions, by faith, in prayer, which is an appeal to heaven. This is a real factor in righteousness, relieving the conscience and real culpability before God. Non-Christians cannot understand such thinking nor can nominal or more Biblically-liberal Christians. Facing death for crimes (which, it must be remembered are tantamount to sins against God) presumably has given many the opportunity to seek salvation in Christ, again a real mitigation. The principle works in the other direction as well. When a court lets a known criminal loose for lack of evidence, it is by faith that since the court exercised responsibility before God, then the Lord will deal with the criminal and the unrequited crime in a providential fashion. No one desires to see anyone put to death, but there is also a strong element of faith and trust in God that the way He has prescribed is the best tack to take in this fallen world.

Objection #3:
Executions give society the message that human life no longer deserves respect.

The following statement in Bedau's words is a typical one used to posit this particular objection:

> Executions give society the unmistakable message that human life no longer deserves respect when it is useful to take it and that homicide is legitimate when deemed justified by pragmatic concerns.[28]

Also, the anti-death-penalty crowd argues, as we previously observed, that lethal injection is *painful* (therefore inhumane), especially at the time the needle is inserted and also at the time the anesthesia begins working. The underlying idea is that no one, not even a murderer, deserves to be put to death. Rae objects,

> This argument suggests that the death penalty is inconsistent with Western civilization's evolving standards of decency and respect for human beings.[29]

Those who hold this position are inconsistent beyond words. Often, the same people who complain about executing convicted murderers fail to complain about abortion, euthanasia, rape, spousal abuse, or other such actions that take life from others. This begs the questions: What about the lives of the victims? Were their lives worthy of respect? The secularists and those Christians who oppose the death penalty have no answer. If secularists are arguing for equality in standards, one has to ask, between criminals and their victims, where is it? Where is the decency and respect for the traumatized lives of those left behind after the murderer has performed his atrocities?

We have seen how the Christian understands that each person is created in the image of God, and yet, nevertheless, the Lord requires the lawful taking of life in specific instances. When God prescribes and commands the death penalty rather than sending the message that human life no longer deserves respect, the exact opposite is the case from a Biblical perspective. That is to say, precisely because Scripture teaches a high degree of sanctity for human life, that does not mean that it teaches an *absolute* view of it. In other words, God prescribes certain instances where it is entirely right, proper, and prudent to take the life of a criminal. God prescribes the means whereby those individuals are to be removed from society, for the overall good of society. Progressive secular humanists actually cheapen life by wanting to play God in abortion and euthanasia, but do not want God to intervene in capital punishment. This is the clear difference between God-ordained and fallen-man-contrived punishment. It is precisely because life is to be valued that society is to be purged of those who do not hold human life to be precious.

Objection #4:
Reliance on the death penalty obscures the true causes of crime and distracts attention from the social measures that effectively contribute to the control of crime.

Dr. Bedau speaks on this point when he concludes that in our country, capital punishment

> epitomizes the tragic inefficacy and brutality of the resort to violence rather than *reason* for the solution of difficult social problems.[30]

Unfortunately, his statement is not supported by concrete facts.

Another death penalty opponent, Jim Wallis, evangelical Christian writer and political activist, agrees with Bedau:

> Few white-collar killers sit on death row, and fewer are executed. And *there is no real evidence that it deters murder; it just satisfies revenge.*[31]

The thinking behind this objection is what I call the "victim mentality." Since many secular humanists believe that human beings are "basically good," morally, they absolve the "victim" (read: convicted murderer) of any responsibility and culpability for the crime they committed. Misplacing the blame, they find fault with the perpetrator's family or family life, while they were being reared, their general environment, background, or a host of other circumstances for *making* the person into a criminal. What they exclude, however, is the truth that others were raised with similar backgrounds and in comparable circumstances and do not commit the same types of heinous crimes. In other words, for progressive humanists – of either the secular or Christian variety – someone or something else is always to blame.

In one sense, this is the faulty reasoning that also encourages us to redistribute wealth. Someone is being disadvantaged and it is not their fault. Therefore, society needs to step in – in the form of government handouts – and rescue the victim. In a provocative article in *The Orange County Register,* Robert J. Samuelson provides us with this insight. Speaking of the plight of the poor, he states,

> By and large, the poor aren't poor because the rich are rich. They're usually poor for their own reasons: family breakdown, low skills, destructive personal habits, and plain bad luck. ("Commentary," Sunday, Nov. 9, 2008, 6.)

It is the personal choices that people make that lead them into a life of crime. Modern leftist society doesn't want to hear that kind of talk, because the politically-correct, victim mentality has conditioned us to think otherwise. What is needed, they argue, are more social measures and increased welfare that will effectively correct the cultural disadvantages some people must face. The social engineers believe that their programs will, somehow, make us all better people. True happiness and utopia are just one more tax increase away.

What we need primarily, however, is not *social* correction, but rather *soul* correction. True social correction, if it accords with Biblical principles of social justice still does not address the soul of the convicted murderer.[32] Social justice implemented by the state is messianic – with a lower case "m" – and amounts to totalitarianism, or at least a kind of social justice that leaves God out of the picture. But as we saw above, it is not the place of the state to deal with heavenly things; that is the province of the church. However, before we can have social correction, we need the kind of soul correction the church offers.

When I speak of the soul of the non-believer, I am not referring to his salvation, but rather a concept, truth, idea, or notion that penetrates to the very marrow of his being that informs him of the gravity of the crime he committed, was convicted of, and for which he will receive the death penalty. This particular concept is closely related to the notion of a deterrent. Man does what is wrong/evil because he chooses to do so. There are plenty of examples of people who came from disadvantaged, dysfunctional families and backgrounds who became great contributors to society and benefited our nation. There are hundreds of men, women, and children who suffered evil at the hands of someone else, were disadvantaged, and struggled – sometimes against almost insurmountable odds – with difficulties in life, who now live, love, and laugh every day because they made the right choices. And they don't commit murder.

True social correction is the direct result of the influence of godliness (through individual Christians) among a community of people seeking to worship and obey God. This type of social correction is not the historical or current "social gospel," but rather leads, under God's gracious hand, to conversion or, at least, the restraint or decrease of evil. The church as an institution provides both assembly and education to encourage that influence through its members.

Objection #5:
Reliance on the death penalty wastes resources.

Secularists and Christians who consider themselves "progressive" argue that capital punishment is "counterproductive as an instrument for society's control of violent crime."[33] Their rationale is that pursuing the death penalty is a waste of the time and energy for the courts, prosecuting attorneys, defense counsel, juries, and judicial and correctional personnel. In short, the death penalty is a veritable and overall waste of time and energy.

While it may be true that the wheels of justice turn slowly and demand time, energy, and resources, isn't doing the right thing worth it?

One might argue that murder, and the theft that often accompanies it, is extremely costly to the community. Sparing the community from evil and protecting it by means of capital punishment releases resources otherwise spent stopping the evil, as well as the cost of lifetime care for the incarcerated. Think also of the exorbitant costs of computer security against malicious hackers as a parallel. Fighting crime is expensive, but the net advantage of ridding society of violent criminals is well worth the effort. It is one thing to "waste" resources on something that is frivolous or unjust. It is another thing to spend resources bringing about justice. Both the accused and the accuser deserve justice.

Objection #6:
*Decent and humane societies do not
deliberately kill human beings.*

Dr. Bedau spells out this position very clearly when he writes:

> An execution is a dramatic, public spectacle of official,
> violent homicide that teaches the permissibility of kill-
> ing people to solve social problems – the worst possible
> example to set for society.[34]

To evaluate the sincerity of someone who takes this position,
we need ask only one question: Does the murder of unborn
babies and viable, late-term babies in the womb also point to the
indecency and inhumanity of our society? If they answer in favor
of abortion and a woman's right to kill her unborn child, they
are being hypocritical and inconsequential in their principles
concerning the *deliberate* killing of human beings.

To say the least, it is strange to realize that the bloodshed
these critics are speaking of is the bloodshed that occurs when
the state executes a guilty criminal who has murdered another human being. They are not speaking of the bloodshed at
the hands of the murderer. Many secularists as well as some
Christians continue to attempt to protect the murderer and
not the victim or the family and friends of the victim. This is
not compassion, but rather a terrible misplacement of morals.
Moreover, decent societies have armed forces and police forces
to kill in order that they might protect innocent citizens against
aggressors.

Objection #7:
*Capital punishment has not been proven
to be an effective deterrent.*

A seventh objection to capital punishment is that it has not
been *proven* to be an effective deterrent. This is a common position

among secularists and Christians who are opposed to the death penalty. Again, I will allow Dr. Bedau to explain his position. He writes that those who support capital punishment do so because "the threat of executions deters capital crimes more effectively than imprisonment. This claim is plausible, but the facts do not support it."[35] Dr. Bedau's claim amounts to "truth by declaration." That is to say, Dr. Bedau *declares* capital punishment not to be a deterrent, therefore it isn't; he hasn't provided supporting data, thus he doesn't prove his point. Of course, progressive secularists tend to think differently from Biblical thinkers and conservatives. For example, when Governor George Pataki of New York came out in favor of the death penalty, the *New York Times* featured an article with the headline, "The Rage to Kill Those Who Kill." From this biased point of view, it is easy to observe how some secularists think about putting convicted murderers to death. At the very least, the headline could have read: "The Rage to Lawfully Execute Those Who Murder." The biased *New York Times* chose, however, to place the execution of a known murderer on the same plane as murder itself, although it used the word "kill" incorrectly. In addition, Thomas Sowell, economist, commentator, and author of dozens of books, says the upshot of such a headline is tantamount to arguing that "It would be wrong for the police to drive above the speed limit to pursue someone who was speeding."

Thomas Sowell calls the argument about the death penalty not being a true deterrent the "grand dogma of the opponents" of capital punishment. Sowell writes that

> A 1959 study on which this dogma was based was so crude that it was laughable. But it told the anointed what they wanted to hear.[36]

What is hidden in the headline is that those who favor capital punishment are people "in a rage." Executing murderers, in their line of reasoning is simply repeating the acts that society condemns. In fact, that is what the article went on to say, using this type of self-contradictory reasoning. He argues that the death penalty is clearly and obviously a deterrent. He writes,

> Moreover, we know that the death penalty definitely deters those who are executed. *The fact that this is obvious does not make it any less important.*[37]

One of the strongest answers to this objection is the one Sowell made above. When there is so much misinformation, it is essential and not all that redundant to reiterate, that in the execution of a convicted murderer at least *one* person has been deterred from committing another crime. As for others who might commit murder, it is correct that we can't say exactly how many people have not committed murder because they considered the gravity of the punishment for that crime. However, one thing we do know – fear can be a great deterrent.

In order to explain this point more fully, allow me to refer to yet another economist, Dr. Isaac Ehrlich of the University of Chicago. Dr. Ehrlich is what is known as an "economic theorist." Ehrlich presented his views on capital punishment to the U.S. Supreme Court. Columnist M. Stanton Evans reported that,

> [Ehrlich] compiled some impressive data, analyzing it according to modern methods of statistics, and concluded that, from 1933 to 1969, every execution of a murderer may have saved as many as seven or eight lives. He explained this on the basis that all human action is based on some assessment of costs and benefits. A predictable use of capital punishment is – or was – a cost of homicide, and when criminals were aware of this, there was a restraining effect upon the number of homicides committed.

Ehrlich's projections led Evans to assert,

> Political activists concerned about the sanctity of life
> should favor, not oppose, the use of capital punish-
> ment.[38]

In the realm of deterrents in general, there is far too much
naïveté on the parts both of secularists and Christians alike.
Criminologist from Florida State University, Gary Kleck, declares
that it is statistically and experientially a

> well-established fact that defensive use of guns is com-
> monplace and effective, and that gun ownership among
> non-criminals therefore has *significant* violence- and
> crime-reducing effects.[39]

In another vignette of insight into how deterrents work generally,
Kleck writes,

> Concerning the felons' attitudes toward armed victims,
> 56% agreed with the statement that "most criminals are
> more worried about meeting an armed victim than they
> are about running into the police," 58% agreed that "a store
> owner who is known to keep a gun on the premises is
> not going to get robbed very often," and 52% agreed that
> "a criminal is not going to mess around with a victim he
> knows is armed with a gun."[40]

My point here is simply that it is time Americans began to
acknowledge the fact that whether the ivory tower liberals want
to admit it or not, there are very powerful deterrents at work
in many areas of life. Does this mean that the application of
the death penalty will completely eliminate all murders? No, of
course not, but beginning to expeditiously execute convicted
murderers on death row will send a clear message to them and
others. Moreover, the ultimate reason for executing a convicted
murderer is not deterrence in the first and primary place. The

reason they are executed is to follow the commands of God and to exercise true justice.

Currently, there are about 600 inmates on death row in my state of California. Yet the three main causes of death among those inmates are old age, suicide, and execution, in that order. Actual execution is a very distant third place. It is hard to prove the veracity of the deterrent objection when no executions are actually taking place. Clearly, God believes that the death penalty, properly administered, is both a deterrent and a proper form of retributive justice for society, because that is what He teaches in His Word.

Objection #8:
The death penalty is too good for a murderer.

This is a criticism defended by many, including a number of popular television commentators – including some conservative ones. They affirm that the death penalty is too good for those who have committed murder because it makes it easy for them. In addition, they contend that life imprisonment without the possibility of parole is a better choice because it is suffering that lasts for a lifetime. Professor Bedau agrees. He writes:

> If, however, a severe punishment can deter crime, then long-term imprisonment is severe enough to cause any rational person not to commit violent crimes.[41]

So, Bedau is arguing for extended cruel punishment as a better deterrent? He contradicts himself roundly.

I respectfully disagree with both Professor Bedau as well as with the radio and TV commentators who hold this view. It is true that death comes quickly and finishes the punishment of the convicted murderer. In Scripture, that is the way the Lord desires it. The Lord God Almighty was perfectly capable of telling us plainly in His Word that it was His will for convicted murderers to be incarcerated until they died of natural causes. The reality is, however, that He prescribed no such thing. The divine mandate is the death penalty for convicted murderers.

The secular situation is further compounded by the reality that a number of appointed judges believe that murderers can be rehabilitated and so they are released on parole after having served only a fraction of their original sentences. In case after case, many of these released murderers, rather than being rehabilitated, have gone out and murdered again (recidivism). Again, in 2008, this problem is multiplied by what is called a "sanctuary city" in the United States, where criminals from foreign countries can hide out without ever worrying about being questioned whether or not they are in the country illegally. Who is ultimately responsible when someone with a rap sheet as long as your arm goes out and murders again? Is the judge to be held responsible? Does anyone know? Does anyone care? Here's the point: continued life, however uncomfortable it may be or not be, allows an evil man or woman the possibility to continue to commit crimes, if not outside a prison, then inside a prison. Which one is the most protective and powerful deterrent?

Some Concluding Comments

There is one more thought that must be expressed here and it has to do either with the number of people murdered or the position of the person(s) murdered. For example, some opponents of the death penalty argue that its usefulness depends on *how many* people are actually murdered. If *one person* is murdered, then the penalty should be life in prison. After the murder of several people, then the penalty increases to life in prison without parole. When a larger number of people, let's say at least ten people, are killed by the same murderer, then the death penalty is appropriate. But who decides how many murders are too many to spare the murderer's life? Isn't a murder a murder (a life taken)? And doesn't murder deserve a fair and lawful punishment? Are we to be partial toward one murderer over another?

Another example of this kind of relative thinking and partiality is the automatic death penalty given in many states to a person who murders a police officer. Let me say that I *highly regard* the work of police officers. I am very grateful for their protection. However, I also believe that the law must show no favoritism. Justice, to be true justice, must be blind. All human beings must be treated equally under the law. So if a police officer is murdered, the appropriate sentence for the convicted murderer is death. That is also true if a pastor, a grocery clerk, an office worker, a student, a homeless person, or anyone else is murdered. The value of human life does not depend on a person's calling or station of life. It is dependent, as we have seen, on man bearing the image of God.

Something quite similar can be said about what we know as "hate" crimes. The irony of the language is that history has been unkind to the phrase in the sense that there is no such thing as a corresponding "love" crime. Crimes are by definition – well, crimes. Conceivably, someone might murder another person because of the color of their skin or because of their sexual orientation. The central point, however, is that a murder was committed and murder constitutes a punishable crime. One would be hard pressed to find an example of murder that was committed with an ambivalent attitude and disposition. Getting sidetracked on the politically-correct notion of "hate" crimes distorts the purpose and objective of Biblical equity and justice.

Misplaced sympathy for the criminal has caused failure in society's ability to "purge the evil from among us." Instead of listening to the Word of God, we have chosen the humanistic path of (supposed) rehabilitation. Our plans to reform convicted murderers have more often led to failure than rehabilitation. A large number of those murderers who are paroled, commit another murder in their lifetime. That is known as recidivism, and the rate is alarmingly high. There are a variety of statistical reports available that indicate increasing rates. In addition, the statistics do not indicate that rehabilitation programs in the prisons reduce the recidivism rate, which runs as high as 67% rearrested for violent crimes after parole or release.

Remember, Scripture teaches that when someone attacks and kills a man, woman, or child who is created in God's image, he or she actually strikes at God. The Lord God does not take attacks on His holy image lightly. The image-bearer and the Image-Giver are connected. That is why there is such serious punishment for murder. Our world will have to answer to the Lord someday for forgetting that men and women are image-bearers. In our misplaced sympathy, we allow evil people to strike at a holy God without just punishment. That is a very sobering thought.

We shall now briefly look at the most popular and common objections to the death penalty among some members of the Christian community.

7

OBJECTIONS FROM
CHRISTIANS WHO OPPOSE
THE DEATH PENALTY

BELOW we're going to take a quick look at the most commonly heard arguments against capital punishment from some more liberal-leaning Christians. I will state here that I find none of their arguments convincing.

Objection #1:
Jesus' ethics and teaching eliminates the need for capital punishment.

Some opponents of the death penalty defend their position by embracing a thing called the "ethics of Jesus." I would include the late John Howard Yoder, theologian and pacifist, Brian McLaren, and those of the Emergent Conversation (*"emerging church"*) movement, Ron Sider, Myron Augsberger, David Gushee, Glen Stassen, and Jim Wallis among the contemporary proponents of this viewpoint. For instance, Yoder believes that *all* use of force, whether individual self-defense or the use of the sword by the state, is prohibited by Scripture. Pacifists like him frequently cite Jesus' words in Matthew 5:39 ("But if anyone slaps you on the right cheek, turn to him the other also.") as imperatives that Christians must not defend themselves.

Let's take a moment and unpack that supposition. We have already seen from Exodus 22:2-3 that it sanctions the killing of a home invader.* But there is a key in the Matthew 5:39 text that ought not to be overlooked. A careful reading of the text states that if someone slaps you on the *right* cheek, the Christian should turn to him the other. Jesus is going on the assumption that most people are right-handed. (There are only a handful of us who are gifted to be left-handed.) Therefore, in order to strike someone facing you on the right cheek with your right hand, you would have to back-hand him. In Jesus' day, such an affront would constitute an insult more than a physical attack. John Frame, therefore, is correct when he says, "The slap on the cheek is a traditional insult, not a threat to life and limb."† We conclude, then, that what the Matthew passage prohibits is not self-defense, but rather vengeance (retaliation against an insult).

The late theologian, Cornelius Van Til, said it best when he wrote that "...the ethics of Jesus literature is essentially non-Christian...." Moreover, "...it is objectionable from the point of view of the scope of Christian ethics.... Accordingly, the 'ethics of Paul' is nothing but the 'ethics of Jesus'." In addition,

> ...It should be carefully noted that when we distinguish between the ethics of Jesus and the ethics of Paul the only meaning such a distinction can carry, if we wish to be true to the Christian interpretation, is that by the ethics of Jesus we signify that part of Christian ethics of which Jesus spoke while He was on earth, while with the ethics of Paul we mean that part of the ethics of Jesus which Jesus taught after He had gone to heaven. Both parts belong to the one great system of ethics which we generally speak of as *Christian* ethics.[1]

---

* It should be emphasized that Frame is correct when he stresses that "Scripture says a lot about the responsibility of the family/state to defend the lives of its citizens, by force if necessary" (Frame, *The Doctrine of the Christian Life*, 692).

† Ibid.

In light of Christian epistemology (the doctrine of *how* you know what you know), Van Til correctly states that the positions of author-pastor McLaren, Wallis, Yoder, and their supporters constitute "a bare theism."[2] Far too many today entertain a vague, nebulous sense of a "Supreme Being" or, among many postmoderns, explain that they are not "religious" but are quite "spiritual." In essence, these folks are being idol factories, fabricating a false god rather than serving and worshiping the true, living God. Yet, even those who claim to be Christians are often far afield in what they teach. Two examples will suffice here.

Yoder asserts,

> If the Mosaic Law is to be obeyed, why [do we] not mandate its injunctions on the Sabbath, the cure for leprosy, slavery, or not wearing wool and linen garments together? (Deut. 22:11).[3]

Reminding us that we no longer live in a theocracy like the Israelites did, he points us to the fact that today the people of God are from various nations, ethnicities, languages, and backgrounds and that the majority of modern governments are secular. Yoder uses these points to argue that our entire social and ethical thought and structure has changed so much, it is illegitimate and impossible to apply Old Testament law to today's culture. However, what he fails to say in his argument is that those very same conditions existed in New Testament times. His hermeneutic reveals quite a bit of confusion about the moral, civil, and ceremonial laws still in use in the New Testament.

Yoder also contends that Genesis 9:6 teaches that Christ's sacrifice on the cross abolished all other sacrifices. This is a "leap" of hermeneutics and is found explicitly nowhere in Scripture. He considers capital punishment a "form of sacrifice" and contends that there is no further need for *any* blood sacrifices to atone for sinful actions, even actions like murder.[4]

I will mention three points in response. First, the Bible often tells us that Jesus came to do the will of His heavenly Father (John 4:34; 5:30; 6:38).

Second, the "ethics of Jesus" people often take the texts they use to defend their position out of context or they improperly compare them to the rest of Scripture. It is wrong to twist the Scriptures to say what we want them to say. For example, Jim Wallis in his book *God's Politics* paints a portrait of Jesus as anti-war, identifies Micah's words with a vision for national and global security, believes that Isaiah wanted a more equitable budget where wealth was redistributed, and knows for certain that Amos was opposed to Enron, albeit anachronistically. Brian McLaren, author, in *Everything Must Change*, follows the same path, identifying Jesus with myriad left-wing political agendas.

Thirdly, as was mentioned above, it is quite odd to say that the Bible teaches that Jesus' sacrifice on the cross makes the death of convicted murderers unnecessary when the Apostle Paul argues in Romans 13 – after the resurrection of Christ – that the state is still tasked with bearing the sword.

Objection #2:
Since those who come to Christ on death row are forgiven by God, we should forgive them too.

When someone makes a profession of faith while facing execution, some will insist that the person in question is forgiven by God and, therefore, should be released. The argument runs like this: If God has granted full restoration and forgiveness, society should follow suit, restoring and receiving the prisoner into the full acceptance he or she deserves.

It is certainly true that a loving and gracious God forgives anyone who genuinely repents of their sins and makes a bona fide confession of faith in Christ. Even a prisoner on death row may be forgiven of all his or her sins by a loving and gracious God, but that does not entail the notion that in such cases all earthly penalties should, therefore, be commuted. Conversion does release us from the *ultimate consequences* (everlasting confinement in Hell) of our sins. However, repentance does not necessarily mean that we will not have to live with the effects or natural consequences of our sins. For example, a man may repent of being a gambler and wasting all his family's money. He may repent, amend his lifestyle and stop gambling all together. However, he and his family may still have to suffer economic pressure for years because of the man's past sinful behavior. A redeemed but convicted murderer should still have to suffer the penalty of his past sinful behaviors. Yet, like the thief on the cross, his death will be his entrance into heaven, for God is a God of mercy. The glory that awaits him far surpasses anything on earth.

Objection #3:
Rehabilitated murderers could do much that is good.

Sometimes evangelical or Biblically-liberal Christians operate under unrealistic notions. Christians can imagine hypothetical conversions of criminals through the preaching of the Gospel and then, in turn, the preaching of the Gospel by those prisoners leading to masses of people who come to know Christ and believe. The operative, speculative word here is "could."

They *could* also conceivably do much that is bad, which is within the realm of possibilities and also a viable scenario. Though there are certainly examples of former inmates being used by God, these are exceptions rather than the rule. Again, we must remember that God is the source of *mercy* and the

93

church is to reflect God's mercy, but the state's task is to execute *justice*. It has not yet been proven convincingly that convicted murderers turn out to be model citizens who leave their criminal ways behind them after rehabilitation. Nevertheless, this does not rule out the possibility that there have been genuine, bona fide conversions of prisoners on death row. For this, we may all praise God and be thankful.

Objection #4:
I feel so sorry that someone has to pay with their life.

People have sympathy for a criminal because he or she will have to pay with their life for the crime they committed. Misplaced emotions lead them to favor sparing the life of a murderer. Misplaced sympathy interferes with executing Biblical justice. What is often missing when we feel sorry for a guilty criminal who must suffer because of his crime, is consideration and sympathy for the losses that the loved ones of the victims face. They are the ones most personally affected and disturbed by the crime. They are also the people who most desire justice. Their loved ones, the victims, paid with their lives. Is there no sympathy for them?

The secular media adds to the confusion for it regularly refuses to reveal the grotesqueness and brutality of murder which is a gory, horrific affair. The colossal suffering of the victim is rarely reported in all the terrifying details. I'm convinced that if people really knew what happened, they would be angry and incensed and not so ready either to champion or take the side of the murderer. The media, however, continues to focus on the murderer and the sufferings he or she endures on death row and, finally, the execution – if indeed that actually happens. Because so many in the media elite are personally opposed to capital punishment, they tend not to provide us with many of the actual details of the vicious manner in which the murder went down and the loss and suffering of the victims and their families.

People who have a defective view of sin have an optimistic view of sinful man. They really believe that even the most depraved person can be rehabilitated. But the Bible gives us a different standard, namely that depravity is real and strikes at the root of man's existence. While many of us would love to live in a peaceable kingdom where there is no death or murder, the cold hard facts point in a different direction. Sin has permeated all of society and we must face reality. There are those among us who do not desire to live according to the law nor do they care about the value of life. Justice requires that we direct our sympathies toward those who suffered the loss of a loved one through injustice rather than toward those who act unjustly.

Objection #5:
If we execute someone in error, we are not upholding the justice that God commands.

Frequently opponents to capital punishment pose the possibility that mistakes could occur in the legal process that would interfere with justice being done. An innocent person could be wrongly convicted of a crime, so they reason. We have already touched on this, but to ensure that we understand, I want to devote just a bit more time to this.

That possibility, indeed, exists because human judgment is imperfect. However, if we refrain from something until the *in*fallibility of human judgment is demonstrated, we'll *never* do *anything*. The possibility of human error exists in every facet of life. Some errors, unfortunately, lead to the death of innocents. However, the presence of the possibility of error and death does not stop us from driving cars, flying in airplanes, sky diving, using sharp knives, going hunting, eating in restaurants, recuperating in hospitals, and a host of other activities. Is human error a good reason for discarding an entire penal system? Don't you think that in all times and in all circumstances, there is and always has been a possibility that someone can make a mistake?

The answer to the last question is "yes." There never was and never will be an infallible human court system. Where judgments are made, errors and mistakes will, no doubt, from time to time occur. The only infallible Judge is the Lord God Almighty who knows the hearts, the minds, and the actions of every human being in the past, the present, and the future. Yet, He, in His sovereign wisdom, has given us a set of Biblical standards for trying difficult cases as well as natural law for the government of mankind. Natural law, however, eventually must be brought back to Scripture, since it is ultimately meaningless apart from the Law of God. Courts and judges were in place in the Old Testament and they were called upon to do their work carefully. Were mistakes made in the Old Testament? Of course they were, but that did not dissuade God from having human beings try human cases of law. Deference to God's Law requires faith, trusting Him to sort out the vagaries and fallibility of human ability. Nevertheless, we must keep in mind that God gave men the responsibility for justice as part of redemption and the preparation for eternity as we observed in a number of Vern Poythress's comments. I'll refresh our memories by one citation:

> Thus we may say that state-supervised punishments present a kind of shadow of God's judgment, while Christians through the gospel present the reality to which that shadow points. That is, Christians present the reality of Christ's penal death and the reality of hell awaiting those who do not put their trust in Christ. *When human beings have injured other human beings, both the shadow and the reality need to be presented.*[5]

It is essential for us to keep this in mind. Man bringing all his faculties to bear in an attempt to execute temporal judgment is part of the vindication of God's wisdom. Ultimately, of course, the whole undertaking is not about man, but about God, His glory, and His provision in cases dealing with capital punishment.

A case in point is found in Deuteronomy 17:8-13, as we observed earlier. We are told that with especially difficult cases involving homicide, legal rights, and assault, the Israelites were to "go up to the place that the LORD will choose," and "come to the Levitical priests and to the judge who is in office in those days, and you shall consult them..." (vv. 7-8). Clearly there is no indication in this text that either the priests or the judges were imbued with *infallibility*. They were fallible men investigating the case and rendering a judgment based on the investigation they conducted while following the guidelines set out by Scripture.

Once they declared their decision, the plaintiff was to

> do according to what they declare to you from that place that the LORD will choose. And you shall be careful to do according to all that they direct you (v. 10).

Verse 11 reiterates the same truth in more specific and forceful language. In the twelfth verse we read:

> The man who acts presumptuously by not obeying the priest who stands to minister there before the LORD your God, or the judge, *that man shall die. So you shall purge the evil from Israel. (Emphasis added.)*

The point of these verses is clear. Fallible men gather evidence, study Scripture, and make the best decision possible. From a Christian perspective it needs to be reiterated that *never* in the history of mankind has the standard of infallibility of judgment really been an issue.

In the New Testament, also, there were human courts and there were mistakes made. But that did not keep Paul from teaching that the state was to judge difficult cases of the law and be the "servant of God" in executing punishment if necessary. Today, we still have a fallible law system in place and human judges who not only make mistakes but, at times, actually act foolishly. Nevertheless, God rules and He brings all things to pass as He ordains it. With Him there is never a "mistake," only something that we may not fully understand. From the Christian perspective, therefore, we must not pretend that all laws will be upheld and executed properly, but we must do all within our power to strive for justice and to live by faith.

8

SUMMARY

AND

CONCLUSION

IN this book, we have investigated the subject of capital punishment from a Christian position. We have argued that there is unity between the Old and New Testaments, leading us to conclude that what God commanded in the older covenant regarding the sanctity of life carries over to the New Testament with the Bible taken as a whole. Also, in the post-flood Noahic covenant, the Lord pronounced that man was created in the image of God and that the murder of a human being would require the shedding of the perpetrator's blood.

In the New Testament, Scripture clearly says that the state has the responsibility, as agents of God, to execute capital punishment on convicted murderers. It was also evident that the state is in possession of a knowledge of good and evil and has the power of the sword to execute justice and, where necessary, to execute murderers.

We have investigated a number of objections to the death penalty raised by secularists and found that in terms of providing a consistent life and worldview as well as a consistent ethic, that these arguments left a great deal to be desired. Moreover, secularists' arguments against the death penalty have no solid basis to pronounce any action "good," "bad," "right," "wrong," or "evil." Although secular humanists do not like to admit it, they truly have no right – no foundational grounds – in their system to pronounce anything as something people "ought" to do.

Christians are not immune to objecting to capital punishment and we have looked at a number of objections raised by Christians, especially those who advocate what has come to be known as the "ethics of Jesus." Since the supposed neutrality of the state is not there in practice, those who want to pit, say, Jesus against Paul or Isaiah end in a "bare theism" and do severe despite to the scriptural accounts which inform us that capital punishment is not only permissible, but is also a legitimate means of protecting society and purging the evil from our midst.

A theme that is found throughout this book is the following: *all murder is killing, but not all killing is murder.* The state may and should execute swift and definitive justice upon convicted murderers, thereby preserving the health and well-being of society. Our modern American society has suffered untold damage from convicted murderers who were released only to murder again. In addition, the American taxpayer has borne the financial burden of tens of thousands of dollars cost per year to keep these convicted murderers on death row rather than execute them. This forms a kind of "double whammy" for the American taxpayer. That is to say, because the government does not execute the convicted murderer as it should, the taxpayer is then further burdened with monetary costs as the convicted murderer remains incarcerated either for life or until he or she is granted parole. My argument here is not primarily directed at the additional costs to the American taxpayer, but rather to point out that when the government fails to put the convicted murderer to death and thus purge the evil from the land that belongs to the Creator, there is an added burden for the land as well. Not only have murderers struck at God by striking one or more people created in God's image, but they may eventually be released and murder again.

In the modern church we are reticent to say what God says for fear of other people and what they may think. In the aftermath of 9/11, some theologians bent over backwards to make certain that no one thought God had *anything* to do with that heinous, cowardly act of men. They did the same thing with the devastating hurricane Katrina. Clearly, it wasn't God who built the city below sea level, but to suggest that He had *nothing* to do with it is simply foolish. While even insurance companies make allowances for an "act of God," many Christians don't and won't. More recently, the collapse of the bridge in Minnesota presents yet another case, and so on throughout history.

Let me give an example of what kind of thinking and acting plagues many contemporary Christians. It is essential as we end this book, that we take the requisite time to ponder God-directed, Christ-honoring, and Spirit-filled ethical decisions. Both our heads and our hearts must be engaged. As we have seen, quite often making ethical decisions requires a great deal of thinking and bringing Scripture to bear on the subject. In the process of our decision-making, it is important that we do not merely emote, but rather that we make a decision that is in keeping with what God teaches us in His Word. When it comes to the death penalty then, the popular Biblically-liberal concept of God (love only, no justice) of some Christians would have us forgive and forget. While this tack might assuage our consciences and cause us to believe that we are acting compassionately, in point of fact, we are acting against the revealed will of God. We have all but forgotten that our sovereign Lord, in addition to being loving, just, righteous, and holy, is also wrathful against sin and is to be feared. Once we jettison the one-dimensional God of "only love" of the modern church and return to the God of Scripture, the events of life are placed into a different perspective for us. Not only do we come to a different understanding of God's steadfast covenant love for His people, but also a better and deeper appreciation of God's absolute sovereignty over every event, situation, and circumstance that comes our way. Allow me to explain what I mean by this.

The Westminster Shorter Catechism (Q/A 4) states that God is a spirit, infinite, eternal, and unchangeable in His being, wisdom, power, holiness, justice, goodness, and truth. Even though this definition is by no means exhaustive, it tells us substantially more about the God of the Scriptures than the mere "God is love" one-dimensional approach. In a great deal of modern Christianity, the richness and robustness of God's character and nature have been diminished by not focusing more on the fullness of His perfections given to us by Scripture. Taking the time to learn more about who God truly is means going daily to His written revelation to us and *listening* to *who* God is and *what He says.*

There is much more to say on the subject of capital punishment than I've been able to say here in this short expanse of space. It is my hope and prayer, however, that what you've read has given you some insight into this issue and that it will spur you on to more study in the Word of God.

Pastor Ron Gleason, PH.D.
Yorba Linda, CA

APPENDIX

How Would Jesus Vote?
A Christian Perspective on the Issues
by D. James Kennedy PH.D. and Jerry Newcombe, D.MIN.

CHAPTER 5

CRIME AND PUNISHMENT
JUDGING THE DEATH PENALTY

For rulers are not a terror to good works,
but to evil.
Do you want to be unafraid of the authority?
Do what is good, and you will have praise from the same.
For he is God's minister to you for good.
But if you do evil, be afraid;
for he does not bear the sword in vain;
for he is God's minister, an avenger
to execute wrath on him who practices evil.

(Romans 13:3–4)

How would Jesus vote – or how would Jesus have us vote – when it comes to the death penalty? Some Christians oppose the death penalty under all circumstances. Other believers argue that the death penalty can be appropriate in some circumstances. However, many people are justifiably concerned that some criminal codes have been extremely harsh and cruel and that some people have been executed because of faulty evidence, poor legal help, or their skin color.

For the last several decades, there has been a move in our culture toward a less vindictive and vengeful approach to dealing with criminals. The old concept of "an eye for an eye and a life for a life" has been slowly passing, being replaced with a more merciful approach. Of course one hopes for constructive change in the wrongdoer – to cure the offender and deter him from future crimes. From this perspective, capital punishment is a practice that must inevitably go, for it is absolutely true that capital punishment has never cured anyone. Furthermore, many have argued there is no definite evidence that it deters murder. The question to be faced is this: is the criminal sick and needing a cure, or is he guilty and needing to be punished?

What shall we say about this relatively modern approach to capital punishment? I think, on the surface, it has a tremendous appeal – a real, emotional appeal. We do not *like* to see anyone killed. We have no desire to see anyone placed in the electric chair or given a lethal injection.

But before we come to a conclusion about which view we should support, we need to understand some of the great issues involved in this decision, issues that underlie the whole subject, issues of which most people are completely unaware.

CONFLICTING VIEWS OF LAW

Many of the laws that are part of our national life spring from Judeo-Christian concepts of right and wrong, including the Ten Commandments. But today in the Western world, we are involved in a tremendous legal revolution. Dr. Hebden Taylor, in his excellent book *The New Legality,* states: "The separation of religion from law is rather the separation of Christianity from law. Christianity has for centuries been the major impetus to legal codes, and Western law has been a manifestation of changing and developing currents of Christian philosophy and theology. Now, however, Christianity is in radical and revolutionary process of disestablishment as the religious foundation of laws, states, and civil governments, and it is being steadily replaced by another religion, the religion of humanity or humanism. The fact that humanism is a non-theistic faith does not make it any the less a religion."[1]

Taylor continues: "In every area of the world there is steady pressure against Christianity and continued attempts to abolish 'discrimination' as to creed by making the humanistic creed the standard of all law with respect to religion, the state, and morality. We are in the midst of a world-wide humanistic legal revolution which is even more radical than the bloody revolutions of humanism."[2]

Not only has this new religion of scientific humanism controlled the development of the Russian state and laws (during the U.S.S.R.), but it is also increasingly becoming the foundation for laws in the United States. Thus, in relation to life issues, we see laws being proposed or passed that incorporate this new "humanistic religion." In many diverse ways, the rights of individuals are changing.

Concerning the matter of capital punishment, the basic

scientific, humanistic approach is that laws should deter and *cure*. This seems a much more benevolent way to view criminals, that is, essentially as patients to be treated. However, C. S. Lewis had this to say on the subject:

> This doctrine, merciful though it appears really means that each one of us, from the moment he breaks the law, is deprived of the rights of a human being. The reason is this. The humanitarian theory removes from punishment the concept of desert [what the criminal deserves]. But the concept of desert is the only connecting link between punishment and justice. It is only as deserved or undeserved that a sentence can be [seen as] just or unjust. I do not contend that the question "Is it deserved?" is the only one we can reasonably ask about a punishment. We may very properly ask whether it is likely to deter others and to reform the criminal. But neither of these last two questions is a question about justice. There is no sense in talking about a just deterrent or a just cure. We demand of a deterrent not whether it is just, but whether it succeeds. Thus when we only consider what will cure him or deter others, we have tacitly removed him from the sphere of justice altogether; instead of a person, a subject of rights, we now have a mere object, a "case" to be treated in a clinic.[3]

In other words, when criminals are treated as patients, it depersonalizes the criminal and reduces him to someone who has no free will. His crimes were motivated by his illness, and therefore he is not responsible but needs to be "reprogrammed."

Lewis worried about the emergence of a therapeutic never-never land into which criminals vanish overnight into institutions for treatment. I believe we should share this concern.

DISTINGUISHING KILLING FROM MURDER

What does the Bible say about the subject? Does not the Bible say, "Thou shalt not kill" (Exodus 20:13, KJV)? And does not this, therefore, forbid the taking of life in capital punishment? So some people claim. Yet if we examine the Scripture more carefully, we see that this cannot be correct. The Hebrew term used here is *ratsach*, meaning murder. It is used in both places in the Old Testament where the Ten Commandments are given. Whenever the commandments are quoted in the New Testament, every case uses the Greek word *phoneuo*, the verb for committing murder. The commandment is actually meant to read, "You shall not murder."

The Ten Commandments are found in Exodus 20. If the commandment "not to kill" means that we should under no circumstances ever take a life, whether in murder or in capital punishment, we are faced with a tremendous inconsistency. For the very God who tells us in Exodus 20 that we shall not kill, in Exodus 21:12 says, "He who strikes a man so that he dies shall surely be put to death."

Does the same God command us not to kill in one chapter and to kill in the next? In Exodus 21:15 we read, "And he who strikes his father or his mother shall surely be put to death." And again in verse 17, "And he who curses his father or his mother shall surely be put to death." In verses 22 and 23, we read that if a person injures a pregnant woman, he also is to be put to death. In all, Exodus 21 references six specific crimes for which God commands the death penalty. Furthermore, in Deuteronomy 32:39, God says, "I kill and I make alive." If killing in any form were a sin, God Himself would be guilty.

In Genesis 9:6, God makes this statement: "Whoever sheds man's blood, by man his blood shall be shed; for in the image of

God He made man." This commandment was given immediately after the flood, when God decided to exercise capital punishment upon virtually the whole earth. Until this point there had been no commandment concerning capital punishment. It is obvious that unless God gives to man the right to take another life, it would be blasphemous on our part to take the lives of others. Yet God is delegating to mankind the responsibility of taking the lives of murderers. This was given to Noah. It is, therefore, for the whole human race and has nothing to do with the Mosaic covenant.

This is all well and good for the Old Testament. Yet did Jesus do away with capital punishment in the New Testament?

Carl F. H. Henry was a well-known writer on Christian personal ethics and a Biblical scholar. He pointed out that in the Sermon on the Mount, "Jesus' emphasis on the sixth commandment unveils the inner spiritual attitude of hate as a wicked sin. But to the Old Testament command he does not add that capital punishment and war are wrong. If that is the sense of the commandment, it must belong to the Old Testament conception. But the Old Testament record cannot be reconciled to this alternative."[4]

Jesus's emphasis is the fact that murder may also be committed in the heart, but He is not changing the basic commandment as it is found in the Old Testament, where capital punishment is not only allowed but commanded by God. I believe the testimony of Scripture is clear. God abhors murder. But under certain circumstances, He permits killing if such deaths further the ultimate causes of life and justice.

WHAT ABOUT DETERRENCE?

Does capital punishment discourage other murderers? Dr. Isaac Ehrlich of the University of Chicago is an economic theorist who presented his views on capital punishment before the U.S. Supreme Court. He compiled some impressive data, analyzing it according to modern methods of statistics, and concluded that, from 1933 to 1969, every execution of a murderer may have saved as many as seven or eight lives. He explained this on the basis that all human action is based on some assessment of costs and benefits. A predictable use of capital punishment is – or was – a cost of homicide, and when criminals were aware of this, there was a restraining effect upon the number of homicides committed. Ehrlich's analysis led writer M. Stanton Evans to declare, "Political activists concerned about the sanctity of life should favor, not oppose, the use of capital punishment."[5]

Is Capital Punishment Constitutional?

The Eighth Amendment of the U.S. Constitution prohibits "cruel and unusual punishment."[6] Some modern thinkers want to redefine capital punishment as cruel and unusual punishment. But the Fifth Amendment implies that there is such a thing as the death penalty: "No person shall be held to answer for a capital, or otherwise infamous crime, unless...."[7] The death penalty was used from the colonial era through the founding era up to the present. Not until the 1960s and 1970s did anybody begin to define capital punishment as "cruel and unusual punishment." If the mode of capital punishment is proven to be cruel, then that is to be changed, as has happened from time to time. Thus, we have graduated from firing squads and hangings and the gas chamber to lethal injection in some states.

A Teaching Moment

Did you ever consider what society teaches about the value of human life by either using or not using the death penalty? Dennis Prager, a Jewish conservative commentator and radio talk-show host, observed, "It is a cosmic injustice to allow a murderer to keep his life."[8] In a recent column, he listed ten reasons he favors capital punishment. Here is reason number two: "Killing murderers is society's only way to teach how terrible murder is. The only real way a society can express its revulsion at any criminal behavior is through the punishment it metes out. If murderers all got 10 years in prison and thieves all got 20 years in prison, that would be society's way of saying that thievery is worse than murder. A society that kills murderers is saying that murder is more heinous a crime than a society that keeps all its murderers alive."[9] In the same column, Prager recounts one of the all-too-common tales of a murderer who was released from prison on a legal technicality—only to murder again.[10]

CONCLUSION

How would Jesus want us to vote on the matter of capital punishment? Opponents of capital punishment want us to believe that He would have us oppose the death penalty under any circumstances. And sometimes they aim their arguments at our emotions rather than our minds.

However, I believe the Bible teaches us that there is a place for capital punishment. Of course, there should be every possible safeguard in the exercise of capital punishment in order to protect the falsely accused from being put to death.

Rather than the death penalty denying man's dignity, it upholds it. When human beings deliberately and cold-bloodedly murder other human beings who are made in the image of God, the murderers have forfeited their right to life. Certainly they should be given the chance to repent and make peace with God, but they also should pay for their crimes, even if that means paying with their very lives.

Only by misunderstanding the Bible and destroying the links between Jesus and His Father in the Old Testament could one conclude that Jesus would oppose the death penalty. We should strive to know the Jesus of the Bible (both the Old and the New Testaments) before we cast our ballots on this important issue.

NOTES

CHAPTER 5 – CRIME AND PUNISHMENT

1 Hebden Taylor, *The New Legality: In the Light of the Christian Philosophy of Law,* (Philadelphia: Presbyterian and Reformed Publishing, 1967), v.

2 Taylor, *New Legality,* vi.

3 C. S. Lewis, "The Humanitarian Theory of Punishment," *Essays on the Death Penalty* (Houston: St. Thomas Press, n.d.), 3, quoted in Taylor, New Legality, 24–25.

4 Carl F. H. Henry, *Christian Personal Ethics* (Grand Rapids: Eerdmans, 1957), 305.

5 M. Stanton Evans, "Statistics Show Case for Capital Punishment," *Human Events,* May 3, 1975, 58. [Based on presentation to the U.S. Supreme Court by Dr. Charles Ehrlich, *economic theorist* from the University of Chicago. – EDITOR.]

6 U.S. Constitution, amend. 8, quoted in *The World Almanac and Book of Facts,* 2003 (New York: World Almanac Books, 2003), 548.

7 U.S. Constitution, amend. 5, quoted in *The World Almanac and Book of Facts,* 2003 (New York: World Almanac Books, 2003), 548.

8 Dennis Prager, "Another Argument for Capital Punishment," WorldNetDaily.com, December 12, 2006, www.wnd.com/news/article.asp?article_id=53331.

9 Dennis Prager, "Another Argument for Capital Punishment."

10 Prager writes, "In 1982, James Ealy was convicted of the strangulation murders of a family – including a mother and her two children. It took the jury just four hours to render the guilty verdict, and Ealy was sentenced to life in prison without possibility of parole. However, his lawyers argued that the police had improperly obtained evidence, and an Illinois appellate court, whose justices acknowledged Ealy was guilty of the murders, vacated the ruling. But without that improperly obtained evidence, Ealy could not be retried successfully, and he was released from prison.

"On Nov. 27, 2006, Ealy strangled to death Mary Hutchison, a 45-year-old manager of a Burger King in Lindenhurst, Ill.

"That woman was killed because many Americans believe that it is better to let a murderer go free than to convict one with evidence improperly obtained.

"Whether that position is right or wrong is not relevant here. What is relevant is this: The people who believe in this policy do so knowing that it will lead to the murder of innocent people like Mary Hutchison, just as I believe in capital punishment knowing that it might lead to the killing of an innocent person. So those who still wish to argue for keeping all murderers alive will need to argue something other than 'an innocent may be killed.' They already support a policy that ensures innocents will be killed."

ENDNOTES

---

1 – INTRODUCTION – PAGES 1–6

1 Sinclair Ferguson and David Wright (eds.), "Ethics," in *New Dictionary of Theology,* (Downers Grove, IL: InterVarsity Press, 1988), 232.

2 John M. Frame, *The Doctrine of the Christian Life,* (Phillipsburg, NJ: Presbyterian and Reformed Publishing Co., 2008), 10.

3 Jochem Douma, *Responsible Conduct, Principles of Christian Ethics,* (Nelson Kloosterman [trans.]), (Phillipsburg, NJ: Presbyterian and Reformed Publishing Co., 2003), 41.

4 Herman Bavinck, *Reformed Dogmatics,* Vol. 1, (John Bolt [ed.] & John Vriend [trans.]), (Grand Rapids: Baker Academic, 2003), 58.

---

2 – A HISTORICAL OVERVIEW – PAGES 7–12

1 John Jefferson Davis, *Evangelical Ethics,* 3d Ed. (Phillipsburg, NJ: Presbyterian and Reformed Publishing Co., 2004), 204.

2 Ibid.

3 William Baker, *Worthy of Death,* (Chicago: Moody Press, 1973), 9. Cited by Davis, 204.

4 Francis Nigel Lee, LL.B., D.JUR., D.C.L., PH.D., TH.D. *God's Ten Commandments: Yesterday, Today, Forever.* (Ventura, CA: Nordskog Publishing, Inc., 2007), 10.

5 John M. Frame, *Christian Life,* 250. See Frame's entire discussion on the place of Natural Law, 242–250.

6 Cesare Beccaria, *On Crimes and Punishments,* (London: Printed for F. Newberry, at the Corner of St. Paul's Church-Yard, MDCCLXXV), 64.

7 Davis, 204.

8 Ibid., 206.

9 Ibid. (*Italics added.*)

10 John Feinberg and Paul Feinberg, *Ethics for a Brave New World,* (Wheaton: Crossway Books, 1993), 127.

11 Ibid.

12 John R. Lott, Jr., *Freedomnomics,* (Washington, D.C.: Regnery, 2007), 111.

3 – THE DEATH PENALTY IN CHURCH HISTORY – PAGES 13–21

1 St. Thomas Aquinas, *Summa Theologica*, Part II-II, question 64, articles 2-3.

2 John Calvin, *Institutes of the Christian Religion*, Vol. 2, (John McNeill [ed.] & Ford Lewis Battles [trans.]), (Philadelphia: The Westminster Press, 1967⁴), 1497 (4.20.10).

3 John Calvin, *Romans*, (Henry Beveridge [ed.]), (Grand Rapids: Baker Book House, 1979), 481-482. *(Emphasis added.)*

4 Ibid. *(Emphasis added.)*

5 Calvin, *Institutes*, 1497. *(Emphasis added.)*

6 Ibid., 1498-1499. *(Emphasis added.)*

7 Ibid., 1499. *(Emphasis added.)*

8 For one of the finest explanations of the similarities and differences between the Old and New Testaments, see Calvin, *Institutes*, Chapters. 10 & 11, 1:428-464.

9 See, for example, Greg Bahnsen, *By This Standard*, (Tyler, TX: I.C.E., 1985), especially 13-28. Compare also Walter Kaiser, *Toward Old Testament Ethics*, 39-56.

10 John M. Frame, *The Doctrine of the Christian Life*, (Phillipsburg, NJ: Presbyterian and Reformed Publishing Co., 2008), 3-5, 10.

11 Herman Ridderbos, Matthew, in the series *Bible Student's Commentary*, (Ray Togtman [trans.]), (Grand Rapids: Zondervan, 1987), 99. See also his doctoral dissertation on Matthew: *De Strekking der Bergrede naar Mattheüs*, (Kampen: Kok, 1936); F. W. Grosheide, *Het Heilig Evangelie volgens Mattheus*, (Kampen: Kok, 1954); William Hendriksen, *Exposition of the Gospel According to Matthew*, (Grand Rapids: Baker, 1973).

12 Francis Nigel Lee, LL.B., D.JUR., D.C.L., PH.D., TH.D. *God's Ten Commandments: Yesterday, Today, Forever.* (Ventura, CA: Nordskog Publishing, Inc., 2007), 48.

13 John Jefferson Davis, *Evangelical Ethics*, 3d Ed. (Phillipsburg, NJ: Presbyterian and Reformed Publishing Co., 2004), 199.

4 – FROM THE OLD TESTAMENT – PAGES 23–44

1 Compare Walter C. Kaiser, Jr., *Toward Old Testament Ethics*, (Grand Rapids: Baker Academic, 1983), 134-135.

2 John M. Frame, *The Doctrine of the Christian Life* (2008), 701.

3 Ibid., 684.

4 Carl Henry (ed.), *Baker's Dictionary of Christian Ethics*, (Grand Rapids: Baker Book House, 1973), 84.

5 Kaiser, 165.

6 W. S. Bruce, *The Ethics of the Old Testament*, (Edinburgh: T&T Clark, 1909), 147-148.

7 John Murray, *The Covenant of Grace. A Biblico-Theological Study*, (Phillipsburg, NJ: Presbyterian and Reformed Publishing Co., 1953), 12-13.

8 John Calvin, *Genesis*, John King (trans.), (Grand Rapids: Baker Book House, 1979), 294.

9 Claus Westermann, *Genesis 1-11*, in the series *Biblischer Kommentar Altes Testament*, (Neukirchen-Vluyn, Neukirchener Verlag, 1976), 625.

10 C. F. Keil and F. Delitzsch, *Commentary on the Old Testament*, Vol. I, (Grand Rapids: Eerdmans, n.d.), 152-153. Martin Luther, quoted in Keil and Delitzsch, 153.

4 – FROM THE OLD TESTAMENT – PAGES 23–44 *(continued)*

11 John Calvin, *Genesis*, 295. Compare W. H. Gispen, *Genesis 1–11*, in the series, *Commentaar op het Oude Testament*, (Kampen: Kok, 1974), 296.

12 Gispen, *Genesis*, 296.

13 Victor Hamilton, Genesis 1–17, in the series, *The New International Commentary on the Old Testament*, (Grand Rapids: Eerdmans, 1990), 314.

14 Keil and Delitzsch, 153.

15 Calvin, *Genesis*, 295-296.

16 Kaiser, 167.

17 Keil and Delitzsch, 153.

18 Frame, *Christian Life*, 685.

19 Gleason Archer, R. Laird Harris, and Bruce Waltke (eds.), *Theological Wordbook of the Old Testament*, Vol. 2, (Chicago: Moody Press, 1980), 860.

20 See Bahnsen, *By This Standard*, (Tyler, TX: I.C.E., 1985), especially 270 ff.

21 Archer, 2:860.

22 Frame, *Christian Life*, 587.

23 E.g. *Bowers v. Devito*, 686 F.2d 616 (7th Cir. 1982), http://caselaw.lp.findlaw.com/data2/circs/7th/063627p.pdf (Oct. 2008).

24 P. C. Craigie, *The Book of Deuteronomy*, (Grand Rapids: Eerdmans, 1976), 251. Compare Lev. 24:10-23, especially v. 13.

25 Ibid. *(Italics added.)*

26 Ibid., 252.

27 J. A. Thompson, *Deuteronomy*, (Downers Grove, IL: InterVarsity Press, 1974), 174.

28 Kaiser, 132.

29 John M. Frame, *The Doctrine of God*, (Phillipsburg, NJ: Presbyterian and Reformed Publishing Co., 2002), 450-451.

30 C. S. Lewis, "The Humanitarian Theory of Punishment," in *Essays on the Death Penalty*, (Houston: St. Thomas Press, n.d.), 3.

31 D. James Kennedy and Jerry Newcombe, *How Would Jesus Vote?: A Christian Perspective on the Issues* (Colorado Springs: WaterBrook Press, 2008), 65.

32 See, for example, Dennis Prager, "Another argument for capital punishment," (December 12, 2006), www.worldnetdaily.com.

5 – FROM THE NEW TESTAMENT – PAGES 45–55

1 Vern Poythress, *The Shadow of Christ in the Law of Moses*, (Brentwood, TN: Wolgemuth & Hyatt, Publishers, Inc., 1991), 155.

2 Ibid., 156.

3 Ibid., 157.

4 Ibid., 158.

5 Ibid., 158-159.

6 Ibid., 160.

7 William Hendriksen, *Romans*, in the series, *New Testament Commentary*, (Grand Rapids: Baker, 1981), 433.

8 John Stott, *Romans*, (Downers Grove, IL: InterVarsity Press, 1994) 340.

9 Poythress, *Shadow*, 171.

6 – ADDRESSING THE SECULAR OBJECTIONS
TO CAPITAL PUNISHMENT – PAGES 57–88

1 cf. Scott B. Rae, *Moral Choices,* (Grand Rapids: Zondervan, 2002), 211.

2 Ibid., 209, 217.

3 Ibid., 215.

4 Hugo A. Bedau, http://ethics.acusd.edu/, 1. "The Case Against the Death Penalty." *(Emphases added.)*

5 Rae, *Moral Choices,* 210.

6 Robert Bork, *The Tempting of America, The Political Seduction of the Law,* (NY: Simon & Schuster, 1990), 243.

7 Bork, in a footnote, cites the following description of the ACLU from Donohue's work: "The ACLU opposes laws outlawing gambling, the use of some narcotics (marijuana use is said to be constitutionally protected), homosexual conduct, pornography, abortion, and suicide. The ACLU thinks that in child custody proceedings, homosexuality may not even be considered by the court in determining the best interests of the child. The organization opposes state regulation of abortion. It thinks that the first amendment requires its distribution free of state interference. The ACLU opposes laws that zone pornographic theaters away from churches and schools as well as laws that allow citizens to have the postmaster remove their names from mailing lists of pornographic material. It opposes metal detectors in airports. It does not favor mandatory incarceration, without the possibility of a sentence of probation, except perhaps for murder or treason and, of course, contends that the death penalty is unconstitutional. The ACLU has sued to have declared unconstitutional: the tax exempt status of churches

and synagogues; the employment of chaplains by Congress, prisons, and the armed services; all displays of nativity scenes on public property; the singing of 'Silent Night' in the classroom; and the words 'under God' in the pledge of allegiance."

8 Bedau, "The Case Against the Death Penalty," 1.

9 Kevin Ring (ed.), *Scalia Dissents,* (Washington, D.C.: Regnery Publishing, 2004), 143.

10 David Forte, Edwin Meese III, & Matthew Spalding (eds.), *The Heritage Guide to the Constitution,* (Washington, D.C.: Regnery Publishing, Inc., 2005), 364.

11 Rae, *Moral Choices,* 211.

12 Kevin Gutzman, *The Politically Incorrect Guide to the Constitution,* (Washington, D.C.: Regnery Publishing Inc., 2007), 191.

13 Ring, *Scalia,* 143,

14 Bork, *Tempting of America,* 4. *(Emphasis added.)*

15 Joseph Story, *Commentaries on the Constitution of the United States,* Vol. 6, (Carolina Academic Press, 1987). This work is a reprint of Story's 1833 edition.

16 Gutzman, 192.

17 Ring, *Scalia,* 144-145.

18 Ibid.

19 David Forte, et al., 363.

20 Ring, *Scalia,* 147.

21 Ibid., 150.

22 Bedau, "The Case Against the Death Penalty," 1. *(Emphasis added.)*

23 See Rae, Moral Choices, 214.

6 – ADDRESSING THE SECULAR OBJECTIONS TO CAPITAL PUNISHMENT – PAGES 57–88 *(continued)*

24 Ibid.

25 Bedau, "The Case Against the Death Penalty." (*Emphasis added.*)

26 Bedau wrote the affirmative article on the subject, "Should Capital Punishment Be Abolished?" in Stephen Satris, *Taking Sides, Clashing Views on Controversial Moral Issues,* (Guilford, CT: Dushkin Publishing Group, 1965), 277, 282.

27 Ernest van den Haag, "The Death Penalty Once More", U.C. Davis Law Review; republished as "Should the Death Penalty Be Retained: Yes," in Satris (ed.), *Taking Sides.*

28 Bedau, "The Case Against the Death Penalty," 2.

29 Rae, *Moral Choices,* 215.

30 Bedau, "The Case Against the Death Penalty," 2. (*Emphasis added.*)

31 Jim Wallis, God's Politics, *A New Vision for Faith and Politics in America,* (San Francisco: Harper, 2005), 303. (*Emphasis added.*)

32 See Walter C. Kaiser, Jr., *Toward Old Testament Ethics,* (Grand Rapids: Baker Academic, 1983), 158-163.

33 Bedau, "The Case Against the Death Penalty," 3.

34 Ibid.

35 Ibid.

36 Thomas Sowell, "The Death Penalty," in *Barbarians Inside the Gate and Other Controversial Essays,* (Stanford, CA: The Hoover Press, 1999), 153-154.

37 Ibid.

38 M. Stanton Evans, "Statistics Show Case for Capital Punishment," *Human Events,* May 3, 1975, citing the work of Dr. Isaac Ehrlich, *economic theorist* from the University of Chicago, in his presentation to the U.S. Supreme Court on capital punishment. As quoted by D. James Kennedy and Jerry Newcombe, *How Would Jesus Vote? A Christian Perspective on the Issues.* (Colorado Springs: WaterBrook Press, 2008), 65.

39 Gary Kleck and Don Kates, *Armed,* (Amherst, NY: Prometheus Books, 2001), 148.

40 Gary Kleck, *Point Blank, Guns and Violence in America,* (NY: Aldine de Gruyter, 1991), 133.

41 Bedau, 4.

---

7 – OBJECTIONS FROM CHRISTIANS WHO OPPOSE THE DEATH PENALTY – PAGES 89–98

1 Cornelius Van Til, *Christian Theistic Ethics,* Vol. III in the series *In Defense of the Faith,* (Copyright den Dulk Christian Foundation, 1971), 13, 14. (*Emphasis added.*)

2 Ibid.

3 John Yoder, "Capital Punishment and the Bible," *Christianity Today,* (Feb. 1, 1960): 348,

4 Ibid., 349.

5 Vern Poythress, *The Shadow of Christ in the Law of Moses,* (Brentwood, TN: Wolgemuth & Hyatt, Publishers, Inc., 1991), 158.

BIBLIOGRAPHY

Aquinas, St. Thomas. *Summa Theologica*, Part II-II, question 64, articles 2-3.

Archer, Gleason, R. Laird Harris, and Bruce Waltke (eds.). *Theological Wordbook of the Old Testament*, Vol. 2, (Chicago: Moody Press, 1980).

Bahnsen, Greg. *By This Standard*. (Tyler, TX: I.C.E., 1985).

Baker, William. *Worthy of Death*, (Chicago: Moody Press, 1973), cited by Davis.

Bavinck, Herman. *Reformed Dogmatics*, Vol. 1, (John Bolt [ed.] and John Vriend [trans.]), (Grand Rapids: Baker Academic, 2003).

Beccaria, Cesare. *On Crimes and Punishments*. (London: Printed for F. Newberry, at the Corner of St. Paul's Church-Yard, MDCCLXXV).

Bedau, Hugo A. *The Death Penalty in America*, (NY: Oxford University Press, 1992).

_____. http://ethics.acusd.edu/, Bedau. "The Case Against the Death Penalty."

_____. "Should Capital Punishment Be Abolished? Yes," in Stephen Satris, *Taking Sides, Clashing Views on Controversial Moral Issues*, (Guilford, CT: Dushkin Publishing Group, 1965).

Bork, Robert. *The Tempting of America, The Political Seduction of the Law,* (NY: Simon & Schuster, 1990).

Bruce, W. S. *The Ethics of the Old Testament,* 2d Ed. (Edinburgh: T&T Clark, 1909).

Calvin, John. *Institutes of the Christian Religion,* 4th Ed. Vol. 2, (John McNeill [ed.] and Ford Lewis Battles [trans.]), (Philadelphia: The Westminster Press, 1967).

_____. *Genesis,* 3d Ed. John King (trans.), (Grand Rapids: Baker Book House, 1979).

_____. *Romans.* (Henry Beveridge [ed.]), (Grand Rapids: Baker Book House, 1979).

Craigie, P. C. *The Book of Deuteronomy,* (Grand Rapids: Eerdmans, 1976).

Davis, John Jefferson. *Evangelical Ethics,* 3rd Edition. (Phillipsburg, NJ: Presbyterian and Reformed Publishing Co., 2004).

Douma, Jochem. *Responsible Conduct, Principles of Christian Ethics,* (Nelson Kloosterman [trans.]), (Phillipsburg, NJ: Presbyterian and Reformed Publishing Co., 2003).

Evans, M. Stanton. "Statistics Show Case for Capital Punishment," *Human Events,* May 3, 1975.

Feinberg, John and Paul Feinberg. *Ethics for a Brave New World,* (Wheaton: Crossway Books, 1993), 127.

Ferguson, Sinclair and David Wright (eds.). "Ethics," in *New Dictionary of Theology.* (Downers Grove, IL: InterVarsity Press, 1988).

Forte, David, Edwin Meese III, and Matthew Spalding (eds.). *The Heritage Guide to the Constitution,* (Washington, D.C.: Regnery Publishing, Inc., 2005).

Frame, John M. *The Doctrine of God,* (Phillipsburg, NJ: Presbyterian and Reformed Publishing Co., 2002).

_____. *The Doctrine of the Christian Life,* (Phillipsburg, NJ: Presbyterian and Reformed Publishing Co., 2008).

Gispen, W. H. *Genesis* 1-11, in the series, *Commentaar op het Oude Testament,* (Kampen: Kok, 1974).

Grosheide, F. W. *Het Heilig Evangelie volgens Mattheus,* (Kampen: Kok, 1954).

Gutzman, Kevin. *The Politically Incorrect Guide to the Constitution,* (Washington, D.C.: Regnery Publishing Inc., 2007).

Hendriksen, William. *Exposition of the Gospel According to Matthew,* (Grand Rapids: Baker, 1973).

_____. *Romans,* in the series, *New Testament Commentary,* (Grand Rapids: Baker, 1981).

Henry, Carl (ed.). *Baker's Dictionary of Christian Ethics,* (Grand Rapids: Baker Book House, 1973).

Kaiser, Walter. *Toward Old Testament Ethics,* (Grand Rapids: Baker Academic, 1983).

Keil, C. F. and F. Delitzsch. *Commentary on the Old Testament,* Vol. I, (Grand Rapids: Eerdmans, n.d.).

Kennedy, D. James and Jerry Newcombe. *How Would Jesus Vote? A Christian Perspective on the Issues.* (Colorado Springs: WaterBrook Press, 2008).

Kleck, Gary and Don Kates. *Armed,* (Amherst, NY: Prometheus Books, 2001).

_____. *Point Blank,* Guns and Violence in America, (NY: Aldine de Gruyter, 1991),

Lee, Francis Nigel, LL.B., D.JUR., D.C.L., PH.D., TH.D. *God's Ten Commandments: Yesterday, Today, Forever,* (Ventura, CA: Nordskog Publishing, Inc., 2007).

Lewis, C. S. "The Humanitarian Theory of Punishment," in *Essays on the Death Penalty,* (Houston: St. Thomas Press, n.d.).

Murray, John. *The Covenant of Grace. A Biblico-Theological Study,* (Phillipsburg, NJ: Presbyterian and Reformed Publishing Co., 1953).

Poythress, Vern. *The Shadow of Christ in the Law of Moses,* (Brentwood, TN: Wolgemuth & Hyatt, Publishers, Inc., 1991).

Prager, Dennis. "Another Argument for Capital Punishment," (December 12, 2006), http://www.worldnetdaily.com.

Rae, Scott B. *Moral Choices,* (Grand Rapids: Zondervan, 2002).

Ridderbos, Herman. *Matthew,* in the series *Bible Student's Commentary,* (Ray Togtman [trans.]), (Grand Rapids: Zondervan, 1987).

_____. *Matthew: De Strekking der Bergrede naar Mattheüs,* (Kampen: Kok, 1936).

Ring, Kevin (ed.). *Scalia Dissents,* (Washington, D.C.: Regnery Publishing, 2004).

Satris, Stephen (ed.). *Taking Sides: Clashing Views on Controversial Moral Issues.* (Guilford, CT: Dushkin Publishing Group, 1965).

Sowell, Thomas. "The Death Penalty," in *Barbarians Inside the Gate and Other Controversial Essays,* (Stanford, CA: The Hoover Press, 1999).

Story, Joseph. *Commentaries on the Constitution of the United States,* Vol. 6, (Carolina Academic Press, 1987). This work is a reprint of Story's 1833 edition.

Stott, John. *Romans,* (Downers Grove, IL: (InterVarsity Press, 1994).

van den Haag, Ernest. "The Death Penalty Once More" U.C. Davis Law Review; republished as "Should the Death Penalty be Retained? Yes" in Satris (above).

Thompson, J. A. *Deuteronomy,* (Downers Grove, IL: InterVarsity Press, 1974).

Wallis, Jim. *God's Politics, A New Vision for Faith and Politics in America,* (San Francisco: Harper, 2005).

Westermann, Claus. *Genesis 1–11,* in the series *Biblischer Kommentar Altes Testament,* 2d Ed. (Neukirchen-Vluyn, Neukirchener Verlag, 1976).

Scripture Index

RON GLEASON, PH.D.

ABOUT THE AUTHOR

Dr. Ron Gleason was born on May 1, 1945 in Charlotte, North Carolina. He attended Myers Park High School and graduated in 1963. From 1963 through 1967 he attended The Citadel in Charleston, South Carolina. While at The Citadel, he was a platoon leader, a member of the Senior Sunday Color Guard, inducted into the Economic Honor Society, was a member of the Dean's List, a Distinguished Military Student, and a member of the wrestling team.

Upon graduation, with a B.S. degree in Business Administration, he entered the U.S. Army as a second lieutenant and was stationed at Fort Knox, Kentucky. His first year in the military service found him as a tank commander of a M60A1 tank platoon. His second and third years he taught tank gunnery in the Weapons Department of the Armor School. He also taught a secret course on the comparison of U.S. and Soviet tanks. He was honorably discharged and given the Army Commendation Medal in January 1970.

From 1970 to 1973 he worked for Pfizer Laboratories in Knoxville, Tennessee, where the Lord called him out of spiritual darkness and into His light.

From 1973 to 1975 he attended Gordon-Conwell Theological Seminary in South Hamilton, Massachusetts, receiving his M.Div. degree Magna Cum Laude. He was also a Byington Teaching Fellow in the Systematic Theology Department with Dr. Roger Nicole and was inducted into the Phi Alpha Chi academic honor society.

Upon completion of his M.Div., he pursued studies at the Free University of Amsterdam and completed his minor in the History of Dogma under Prof.dr. Jan Veenhof, the successor of Prof.dr. G.C. Berkouwer.

He was granted a full government scholarship from the Dutch government and transferred to the Theologische Hogeschool van de Gereformeerde Kerken in Nederland, (Theological Seminary of the Reformed Churches in the Netherlands) located in Kampen, in mid-1977. There, he completed his New Testament minor with Prof.dr. Herman N. Ridderbos as well as his major of Systematic Theology and Ethics with Prof.dr. J.T. Bakker. He received his doctoral degree with honors in 1979. He also worked as a theological assistant to Dr. Bakker from 1979 to 1981.

Dr. Gleason holds an earned Ph.D. in Systematic Theology from Westminster Theological Seminary in Philadelphia, Pennsylvania. His mentors and study leaders were Sinclair Ferguson and Richard Gaffin. His dissertation was on the centrality of the mystical union of the believer with Christ (*unio mystica*) in the theology of Dr. Herman Bavinck (1854–1921).

He was ordained in the Gereformeerde Kerk (Reformed Church [Article 31]) in The Hague in 1981 and served as the pastor of a Dutch speaking church from 1981 to 1985 in Rijswijk, Holland.

From February 1985 through August 1994 he served as pastor of Bethel Canadian Reformed Church in Toronto, Ontario.

While there, he organized the Toronto Conference on Reformed Theology, started a group for victims of sexual abuse, and was on the board of Ligonier Ministries of Canada.

He is currently the pastor of Grace Presbyterian Church (PCA) in Yorba Linda, California.

He has lectured internationally at the Freie Evangelish-Theologische Akademie in Basle, Switzerland, Het Evangelish Instituut, in Haverlee, Belgium, and the Reformatorische Bijbel-school, in Zeist, Holland. He has also lectured at Westminster Theological Seminary in Philadelphia, Pennsylvania, Westminster Theological Seminary in Escondido, California, Reformed Theological Seminary, in Orlando, Florida, at Biola University in La Mirada, California, and at Reformed Theological Seminary in Memphis, Tennessee.

He has been married to Sarah Yopp Gleason for forty-one years and has six children, one of whom is with the Lord. He lives with his family in Orange, California. Sally and Ron have been blessed with twelve grandchildren.

Dr. Gleason reads or speaks Hebrew, Greek, Latin, Dutch, German, Afrikaans, Spanish, French, and a little bit of English. He publishes a weekly ethical newsletter entitled *Ethos*. His articles are posted on numerous Web sites.

He has served on the board of Growing Reformed Churches of the Southern California Reformed Fellowship. He is past chairman of the Candidates and Credentials Committee, the Christian Education Committee, and presently the Stated Clerk of South Coast Presbytery of the PCA. He was inducted into the Heritage Foundation's "Who's Who in America" in 2004. He is the President of California Exodus, an organization that encourages parents to remove their children from public schools.

He has written two children's books entitled *The Little Lieutenant* and *Andy's Summer Adventure*. He is currently working on three more books. The first is about baseball based on his son's being drafted out of high school by the New York Yankees, which will chronicle the ups-and-downs of baseball. The second is about The Citadel and will be entitled *End as a Man*. Finally, he's writing one about amateur wrestling called *Near Fall*.

Academically, he has submitted an ethical work on Capital Punishment as well as an entire series of ethical commentaries aimed at the man and woman in the pew. He is the editor of *Reforming or Conforming?: Post-Conservative Evangelicals and the Emerging Church* (2008 Crossway). He is also under contract with Presbyterian and Reformed Publishing Co. for a biography of Dr. Herman Bavinck, a Dutch theologian, which is scheduled to be released in 2009. Ron will be a co-editor on the upcoming *Festschrift* for Dr. David Wells. Work has also begun on a practical work dealing with who God is with the tentative title of *Who Is the Lord That We Should Worship Him?* He hopes to continue to write on Presbyterian and Reformed social ethics. He and his wife are co-authoring a book on Christian marriage based on the couple's twenty-seven years of experience in pre- and post-marital counseling.

Ron has contributed to popular magazines and technical scholarly journals in Holland, Canada, and the United States. Many of those articles can be found on his Web site at http://www.rongleason.org. His blog site is http://rongleason.blogspot.com. He has also frequently spoken at various conferences. Ron can be contacted by email at bavinck@socal.rr.com, or phone 714.692.2390 (Church), or in care of Nordskog Publishing.

ACKNOWLEDGMENTS

IT is with a great deal of joy that I take a few moments and thank those who have been so helpful and such an encouragement to me on this writing project. Someone told me recently that writing and publishing books is like giving birth to barbed wire. While quite graphic, there is an element of truth in that description. Simultaneously, although books are conceived and written by the authors, that is not to say that others do not have a hand in the work.

First, I want to thank one of my best critics and the love of my life, my dear wife, Sally. God has blessed me with an awesome Christian woman, who shows me daily what it means patiently and faithfully to keep your wedding vows. Though my Sarah may be married to a difficult man, she is, however, as her name says, a Princess – in the good sense of the word. Her suggestions, corrections, and improvements have been invaluable in helping me get this book ready for publication.

Second, thanks are due to my children, daughters-in-law, and grandchildren: Ron, Geoff, Janneke, Nicoline, and Hans; Jennifer, Lisa, and Blanca; and Laura, Avery, Cailen, Cole, Rachel, Laken, Naya, Sawyer, Noel, Marin, Emma, and Charlotte. You are all a blessing and inspiration to me.

Third, the Lord has given me a true "Band of Brothers" at Grace Presbyterian Church with my fellow Elders: Tom Curtis, Jim Dailey, Don Huizenga, Doug MacLeith, Rob Olson, Dana Randall, Herb Seigler, Andy Szemerei, Rob Watson, and Russ

Young, and our Deacons: Richard Butler, Brian Chicoine, Mike Delgado, Vic Lin, Don Penksaw, Brian Peters, Ray Sahagun, and Bill Selvig.

Fourth, special thanks are in order for Devon Dailey, the church secretary. I could not ask for a more efficient and patient helper at the church office. She still doesn't believe that things are going to slow down next week and she is living with my motto: Yesterday was the easy day. Thank you so much for what you do for me and God's people!

Fifth, I must say a word about the members at Grace Presbyterian Church. They have been one of the driving forces behind this book with their questions and hunger for God's Word. I cannot begin to express my appreciation for the love, harmony, unity, and covenant community spirit that dominates at Grace and each one of you has played an integral part in making Grace Presbyterian Church a very special place to minister the Gospel of Jesus Christ.

Finally, I want to express my thanks to Jerry Nordskog, Desta Garrett, Ron Kirk, Bayard Taylor, and Kimberley Winters Woods for their insightful editorial comments. This book would not have been nearly as good, organized, cogent, and coherent without their help and editing enhancements. Thank you all so much.

It is my prayer that this book will prove to be of value to all who read it – Christians and non-Christians alike and that it will serve to further the discussion about capital punishment in our society. Most importantly, I pray that this book will bring honor and glory to the God who called me out of darkness and into his marvelous grace. His grace helps me understand the Latin phrases, *Post tenebras lux!* and *Soli Deo Gloria!*

Pastor Ron Gleason, PH.D.
Yorba Linda, CA
Thanksgiving Day 2008

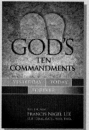

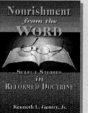

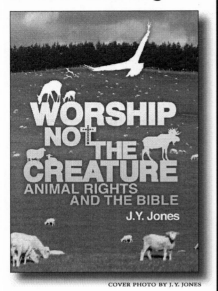

PHOTO BY LINDA JONES

J. Y. JONES, M.D. His ninth book, *Worship Not the Creature*, follows more than 250 published articles, six non-fiction books, and a soon-to-be published third novel. An avid hunter, Dr. Jones has taken all North American big game species using the same Remington .30-06 rifle, resulting in the book *One Man, One Rifle, One Land* (Safari Press, 2001); and he's close to repeating this with the Erasian sequel, *Another Rifle, Another Land*. Dr. Jones helped Safari Press produce the *Ask the Guides* series, their most successful North American hunting books. Dr. Jones has been an eye physician and surgeon for four decades. He is a decorated Vietnam veteran, speaks Spanish and Russian, and has volunteered in twenty-three overseas eye-surgery mission trips. He has received numerous awards for writing and photography, and is a frequent speaker at sportsmen's events, where he particularly enjoys sharing his Christian testimony. J.Y. and Linda have been married since 1964.

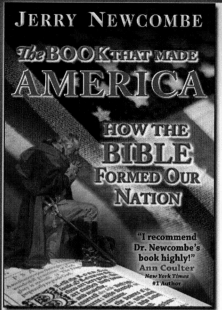

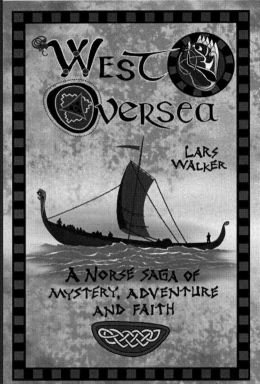